Call It Experience

———

ERSKINE CALDWELL

Call It Experience

THE YEARS OF LEARNING
HOW TO WRITE

Foreword by Erik Bledsoe

BROWN THRASHER BOOKS

THE UNIVERSITY OF GEORGIA PRESS

ATHENS AND LONDON

Published in 1996 as a Brown Trasher Book
by the University of Georgia Press, Athens, Georgia 30602
© 1951, 1979 by Erskine Caldwell
Forword to the Brown Thrasher edition © 1996
by the University of Georgia Press
www.ugapress.org

Most University of Georgia Press titles are
available from popular e-book vendors.

Printed digitally

Library of Congress Cataloging in Publication Data
Caldwell, Erskine, 1903–
Call it experience : the years of learning how to write / Erskine
Caldwell ; forword by Erik Bledsoe.
xv, 239 p. ; 22 cm.
"Brown Thrasher books."
Originally published : New York : Duell, Sloan and Pearce, 1951.
ISBN 0-8203-1849-3 (pbk. : alk. paper)
1. Caldwell, Erskine, 1903–1987—Childhood and youth.
2. Novelists, American—20th century—Biography.
3. Authorship. 4. Southern States—Social life and customs. I. Title.
PS3505.A322Z463   1996
813'.52–dc20
[B]   96-865

Biritish Library Cataloging in Publication Data available

ISBN-13: 978-0-8203-1849-3

Foreword

ERIK BLEDSOE

What, I have sometimes wondered, is the reader's fascination with autobiography? Why did you pick up this book, this autobiography of Erskine Caldwell, instead of one of his novels? Likely, you have already read one or more of the books or stories that brought Caldwell fame and justified his writing *Call It Experience*. And if you are similar to me, you turned to Caldwell's autobiography in hopes of gaining a better understanding of the mind that created Jeeter Lester, Ty Ty Walden, Pluto Swint, and that horrifying scene in the hog pen from "Kneel to the Rising Sun." But my fascination with literary autobiography goes beyond the individual whose work I am reading. When I read an autobiography of a writer, I am seeking to understand not only how that person became an artist but also the creative spark within all artists, the innate urge and ability to make art.

A reader who shares my interests is likely, at first glance, to be disappointed in *Call It Experience*. In comparison to some other literary autobiographies, Caldwell does not seem to give his reader much insight into his work. In *One Writer's Beginnings*, for example, Eudora Welty discusses with both example and definition the notion of *confluence*, which she suggests is at the heart of her creative process and all of her fiction. Erskine Caldwell offers his readers no such key to his creativity. Indeed, he seems at times to be deliberately bursting the romantic bubble that I and others have of writers—that they belong to a mysterious realm open only to special people who allow the rest of us to visit awhile by reading their work. With just a touch of sarcasm, Caldwell begins his preface by stating that he wrote this book for "curious readers and would–be authors who seek visions of the wonderland in which all authors are believed to exist." If such a wonderland exists, Caldwell suggests in *Call It Experience*, the author does not arrive there by chance as Alice did but rather through long hours, days, and years of hard work. There is no magic involved in authorship, only long years of learning how to write, as Caldwell's subtitle claims.

For Caldwell, becoming a writer meant "sitting cramped and ill humored all day or all night at a desk and typewriter." It meant sacrifice and effort. In its advocation of a puritan work ethic, *Call It Experience* more closely resembles Benjamin Franklin's *Autobiography* than Welty's *One Writer's Beginnings*. Often considered the archetypal American autobiography, Franklin's book is one of the earliest and most powerful rags–to–riches stories. It is no accident that *Call It Experience* begins with Caldwell's childhood as the son of a poor minister in the South, follows him through several low-paying jobs, and ends with him signing books for lines of admiring and, more important, paying fans in Kansas City. Even if Caldwell never read Franklin's autobiography, he absorbed the statesman's message as did the rest of society: success in America is measured not by where you start but by where you end up, and the farther from where you began the better. In *Call It Experience*, Caldwell sets out to tell his version of the American success story, not to bare his creative process or to reveal intimate details about his private life.

Indeed, Caldwell was a very private man—taciturn in conversation, more comfortable watching others at a party than being the center of attention. The photographer Margaret Bourke-White, who would become Caldwell's second (but not final) wife, described her first impression of him: "His whole appearance suggested he was holding himself ready to step back at any moment and blend into the background, where he would remain, patient and invisible, until he had heard what he wanted to hear or experienced what he wanted to experience."[1] While such introversion may have made Caldwell a better observer of people and consequently a better novelist, it is not the most desirable quality in an autobiographer. The editor with whom Caldwell worked on his second autobiography, *With All My Might*, published only a few weeks before Caldwell's death in 1987, once told me a story that perfectly illustrates how much Caldwell valued his privacy. After reading the manuscript, the editor wrote to Caldwell and requested that he add more details about how his parents' deaths affected him since the events were only briefly mentioned in the book. Caldwell sent back a tersely worded note that read in part: "The book is as I intended it to be."[2]

Caldwell's autobiographical writings often leave readers and editors wanting to know more about the author, and this sense of longing may cause readers of *Call It Experience* to feel disappointed. Actually, Caldwell does reveal a great deal about himself in this book, although not in a conventional manner. To discover the man behind the public figure we must emulate Caldwell by standing back, observing quietly, and carefully listening not only to what he tells us but also to the way he tells us, all the while noting those subjects he does not address.

Before affirming certain truths about Caldwell in *Call It Experience*, we must acknowledge certain untruths that emerge not from his desire to deceive but through faults of the "memoranda and memory" technique that Caldwell used to write his memoirs. For example, Caldwell claims he and his parents moved to Wrens, Georgia, in 1918. In reality, that move did not occur until the summer of 1919. There are other discrepancies in *Call It Experience*, though not as many as in *With All My Might*, which was written much later. Time clouds the memory, and details are sometimes blocked from the writer's eye. Such factual mistakes are easily forgiven; it is the job of the biographer to authenticate the record with stacks of letters, newspapers, and other documents of a life lived. However, from the autobiographer we expect to learn what the biographer can only speculate about—the insights and perspective of the person who lived the life.

Several omissions in *Call It Experience*, deliberate or not, may strike the reader as odd while further revealing Caldwell's guarded nature. For example, he never mentions outright his marriage to Helen Lannigan while he was a student at the University of Virginia. Their union is merely alluded to by Caldwell's shift to the plural pronoun "we" when describing his life in Maine. Yet he never explains who "we" may be and never refers to Helen by name. Caldwell's three children from the marriage are mentioned only indirectly as he describes his efforts to provide for a "family of five persons." Certainly, no autobiography can be all inclusive, and in his preface Caldwell freely admits that "[i]t has not been my intention to put down in detail all the happenings of my lifetime but to relate to some extent those experiences that may have contributed to my writing and may have been reflected in short stories and novels." However, even with such criteria for admission, Helen's exclusion seems unjustified. Caldwell often turned to her for editing and advice during his early years of writing. The extent of her influence is demonstrated best in a letter he wrote to her in 1932 while in New York, desperately trying to rewrite the fatally flawed manuscript of *Autumn Hill*. Caldwell wrote *Autumn Hill* immediately after *Tobacco Road*, and Scribner's rejection of it prompted him to leave that publishing house and the editorial guidance of Maxwell Perkins. But before he made that decision, he rented a room in New York and tried to revise the novel according to Perkins's suggestions. "I am depending on you, though," Caldwell wrote to Helen in Maine, "to tell me if the new part is fine enough. Without your help I couldn't do anything with it. I never know until you tell me."[3]

Certainly, the omission of Helen is due in part to her status as ex–wife at the time Caldwell wrote *Call It Experience* and in part to Caldwell's private nature. He probably wanted to avoid dredging up old grievances and the possibility of a lawsuit. But, the omission also illustrates the degree to which Caldwell needed to be seen as a self–made man, someone who recognizes what he wants and sets out to achieve it with little help from anyone else. Georges Gusdorf, one of the preeminent theorists of autobiography, reminds us that an autobiography presents its author "not as he was, not as he is, but as he believes and wishes himself to have been."[4] In *Call It Experience*, Caldwell presents himself as being nearly self–created. Consequently, people who greatly influenced him and his writing are at times omitted, such as Professor Atcheson Hench at the University of Virginia, or their significance is understated. Even his father, the Reverend Ira S. Caldwell, the greatest influence in Caldwell's life, barely appears in this work, and his death is not mentioned at all.

The most moving homage Caldwell pays to an influence in *Call It Experience* is to Max Perkins, the legendary editor at Scribner's. The scene where Caldwell decides to change publishers and stands outside Scribner's while looking up at Perkins's office is one of the few times Caldwell allows private emotion to enter his story. The scene speaks (albeit quietly) a great deal about the love and respect Caldwell felt for his editor.

Scenes with Perkins are perhaps the most memorable in the book, and certainly the best of these is the phone conversation in which Perkins informs the young writer that he wants to publish two of his stories in *Scribner's Magazine*, Caldwell's first sell to a major magazine. This anecdote represents one example of Caldwell relating a different version of what truly occurred. While I do not want to spoil the punch line for those who have not read the story, I will say that the phone conversation certainly never occurred as reported. Caldwell was not as naive as he portrays himself in that scene. Caldwell has that trait common to many a good

southern storyteller; he is never willing to let the facts inter-
fere with a good tale. Readers are willing to forgive this "in-
accuracy" because—well, frankly, because it is a funny story,
true or not.

The phone conversation with Perkins is but one of the
many times Caldwell chooses to present himself as being a
bit naive, a bit of the country bumpkin in the big city. Other
examples of this tendency are seen when Caldwell recalls
the time his valuable first edition of *Sister Carrie* was stolen
by an unscrupulous New York book dealer and the time he
was seduced by the unnamed woman in Kansas City. In these
scenes, in this depiction of himself, *Call It Experience* again
reminds us of Benjamin Franklin's *Autobiography*—where the
author humorously recalls his own naive arrival in Philadelphia, walking the streets wide-eyed and munching on bread
while stuffing extra loaves into his pockets. Franklin's inaus-
picious arrival only makes his eventual success in the city
that much more dramatic. So too with Caldwell. He is the
largely uneducated rube who arrives on the literary scene
only eventually to conquer it.

In *Call It Experience* Caldwell tells the story of his rise to
fame in the literary world. The various poses he adopts for
himself as he makes that journey (naive small-town boy in
the big city, self-trained artist, and others) are devices used
to promote a dramatic view of his life, which is not to say
that they are untruthful (at least not always), but only that
Caldwell chose to reveal certain truths for a particular reason, exaggerating stories at times for effect while omitting
other items that did not conform to the pattern he wanted
to develop.

Foreword

One final issue that should be explored is why Caldwell chose to write his first autobiography when he did. Georges Gusdorf suggests that the majority of autobiographies are written by people at the end of their careers "in order to celebrate their deeds (always more or less misunderstood), providing a sort of posthumous propaganda for posterity that otherwise is in danger of forgetting them or of failing to esteem them properly."[5] But in 1951, Caldwell's career was far from over, particularly if judged by production. He would publish more than two dozen books after *Call It Experience* and before his death. His books would continue to sell hundreds of thousands, even millions, of copies in paperback. Few writers ever achieve the financial success that still awaited Caldwell after *Call It Experience*.

Yet in spite of the marketing phenomenon, many believed Caldwell's talent had been exhausted. While readers continued to buy his books, many enticed by the scantily clad women that inevitably showed up on the covers, most reviewers and critics had given up on him as a writer of serious literature. In a 1948 review of *This Very Earth*, *Time* magazine declared "Caldwell's Collapse." The reviewer used only the past tense to discuss Caldwell's talents and said "each of his recent novels is more inept than its predecessor, and the latest one is as scrawny a literary turkey as has been hatched in 1948."[6] Although William Faulkner had once declared Caldwell to be one of the top five living American authors, by the mid–1950s he too would say that while Caldwell's work in the 1930s had been very good, his later work "gradually grew towards trash."[7]

Foreword

Such comments stung Caldwell. He claims in *Call It Experience* and elsewhere that after reading the reviews of *American Earth*, his first collection of stories, he no longer cared what critics thought of his work, that he wrote only for himself and his readers, but the statement is a hollow one. Throughout his life he filled scrapbooks with review clippings, and his letters to friends during the 1930s are filled with comments on how his books were being reviewed. When critics praised him, as they often did during the 1930s, he was pleased; when he lost their favor he suffered. He dealt with this pain by denying it and claiming he did not care what they said. *Call It Experience* is Caldwell's public retaliation directed at critics who had rejected him. He ends his autobiography with the story of being snubbed by other writers and academics at a literary conference because he had arrived there after signing paperbacks for fans in a drugstore, behavior that the conference participants thought demeaned the profession of writing. In this story the point is clear: Caldwell cares more for his fans than for reviewers, academics, and other writers, or so he claims. He crafts himself as the literary outsider, but above all, *Call It Experience* is Caldwell's effort to convince others, and himself, that his career is not over.

While Caldwell may seem stingy at times with details about his life in *Call It Experience*, when we examine the details he does give us we see a fuller portrait of the man than we first suspected was present. In autobiography, Gusdorf reminds us, "there is truth affirmed beyond the fraudulent itinerary and chronology, a truth of the man, images of himself and

the world, reveries of a man of genius, who, for his own en-
chantment and that of his readers, realizes himself in the
unreal."[8] We must read autobiography not as a mirror of the
life, but rather as the author's comment upon that life. Even
as Caldwell attempts to hide one part of his life from the
reader's prying eyes he cannot help but reveal another facet.
On the surface *Call It Experience* is a celebration of literary
achievement, but underneath it contains the author's fear of
failure. As Caldwell guides us through "the wonderland in
which all authors are believed to exist," we learn, as did Alice,
that wonderlands can be unpredictable and illusory places.

This self–portrait of Caldwell reveals more about him than
he might have realized or have been willing to reveal. It is
this underlying anxiety, this tension between the best-
selling writer and the author who longed for critical success,
that ultimately makes *Call It Experience* a satisfying read; for
it is within this tension that we discover the real Erskine
Caldwell, the person behind the public persona he so carefully crafts in this autobiography.

NOTES

1. Margaret Bourke–White, *Portrait of Myself* (Boston: G. K.
Hall, 1985), 114.

2. Chuck Perry, conversation with author, October 1992.

3. Erskine Caldwell to Helen Caldwell, undated letter (late
March or early April 1932), Erskine Caldwell Collection, Special
Collections, Baker Library, Dartmouth College, Hanover, N.H.
I thank Dartmouth College Libraries for allowing me access to

this material and McIntosh and Otis, Inc., for permission to quote from it. Quotation from the unpublished letter of Erskine Caldwell, © 1996 by Virginia Caldwell Hibbs. Reprinted by permission of McIntosh and Otis, Inc. No further use of this material is permitted without obtaining permission through McIntosh and Otis, Inc., 310 Madison Ave., New York, NY 10017.

4. Georges Gusdorf, "Conditions and Limits of Autobiography," trans. James Olney, in *Autobiography: Essays Theoretical and Critical*, ed. James Olney (Princeton: Princeton UP, 1980), 43.

5. Gusdorf, 36.

6. "Caldwell's Collapse," *Time*, 30 August 1948, reprinted, in *Critical Essays on Erskine Caldwell*, ed. Scott MacDonald (Boston: G. K. Hall, 1981), 86.

7. William Faulkner, *Faulkner at Nagano* (Tokyo: Kenkyusha, 1956), 58. For Faulkner's earlier praise of Caldwell see Joseph Blotner, *Faulkner: A Biography* (New York: Random House Inc., 1974), 2:1213.

8. Gusdorf, 43.

Preface

The purpose of this volume is to set forth some of the experiences of an author which may be of interest to curious readers and would-be writers who seek visions of the wonderland in which all authors are believed to exist.

It has not been my intention to put down in detail all the happenings of my lifetime but to relate to some extent those experiences that may have contributed to my writing and may have been reflected in short stories and novels. What is to be found here is less a personal history than it is an informal recollection of authorship.

Some things have been left out unintentionally; other things have been omitted purposely. For instance, I feel that no purpose would be served in relating my experiences as a Y.M.C.A. chauffeur at Millington Air Field in Tennessee during the First World War, as a field hand picking short staple cotton in Alabama in the Nineteen Twenties, as a passenger in an airplane that was struck by lightning over Arizona in 1942, or as a tourist who won twenty-seven thousand francs playing roulette at the casino in Monaco in 1949.

This book was written from memoranda and memory

Preface

and it has been my intention to recall incidents and conversations to the best of my ability. If any reader should find me to be in error in any respect, I shall be grateful if such mistakes are brought to my attention so that corrections can be made in any subsequent edition of this book.

Contents

Contents

Call It Experience

Part One: The Early Years

I.

Probably almost everyone who makes his bread as a storyteller has at some time asked himself how it happened that he did not become an actor or a banker or a shoe salesman but became instead an author.

The more rational-minded, or at least those with a better memory, perhaps can easily recall some youthful and zestful incident that actually determined such a turning point in their lives. I am not so fortunate. I am one who even now often wonders what happened twenty-five or thirty years ago that so decisively guided, induced, or pushed me into the way I have taken.

I can be sure that writing short stories and novels was not something I could do effortlessly and gracefully. I moved about awkwardly at the task and felt ill at ease when confronted by the results. The physical act of writing fiction went against the grain. It meant sitting cramped and ill humored all day or all night at a desk and typewriter when I wanted to be up and going somewhere to see something I was convinced was more interesting than what I was doing. It meant trying to create lifelike people and meaningful events within the narrow confines of the small world I knew. It meant striving to put into words on paper the elusive feeling and spirit of life—an endless reaching for precise meanings and shades of meanings—and more often than not I had difficulty when it came to spelling correctly the name of a common household pet.

And certainly I did not have writing thrust upon me. No teacher ever suggested that I look to authorship as a career. No journeying editor or publisher, prepared to smile upon a fair-haired boy, stopped by. My mother hoped I would seek a traditional profession, and urged me to prepare myself for the study of law or medicine; my father, although I do not remember his ever mentioning it, probably would not have been disappointed if I had entered the ministry.

As well as I can recollect, now that I am in my middle forties, I had no desire, no urge, no inclination to be a writer when I was growing up between the ages of twelve and sixteen. But evidently something did happen, about the time I was fifteen or sixteen or seventeen, and when I got to be twenty-one or twenty-two, I realized I wanted to write more than do anything else in the world. Not long afterward I confidently made up my mind to make my way as an author, with no sidelines attached, to the end of life. The first goal I set out to reach was that of becoming a published fiction writer within ten years' time. It was an easy vow to make, and I soon learned that wishful thinking was not enough. I was able to acquire the necessary determination and stubbornness of mind, but the ability remained elusive for a long time.

I think one of the important lessons I learned during

those early years was that life itself was to be my most consistently rewarding teacher. Call it experience, if you will; but whatever it is called, I have been seeking it ever since.

2.

I was in my fifteenth year, the time being 1918, when I learned that under certain conditions money could be earned by work, and that labor under other circumstances did not necessarily produce pay. My parents had moved to Wrens, Jefferson County, Georgia, a small town of twelve hundred persons in the sand-clay cotton country thirty miles west of the Savannah River, where my father, the Reverend Ira S. Caldwell, was the pastor of the Associate Reformed Presbyterian church. Before that we had lived for several years near Atoka, Tipton County, Tennessee, a small farming community north of Memphis and not far from the Mississippi River, where my father had been pastor of the Salem A.R.P. church. Prior to that time we had lived in many places in the Carolinas, Virginia, and Florida, because of the fact that since my birth, December 17, 1903, in Moreland, Coweta County, Georgia, my father had been secretary of the A.R.P. Home Missions Board.

I had been attending high school in Wrens for several months when I found out that several of the older boys in school had part-time jobs at the cottonseed oil mill. I went to see the foreman who, after looking me over,

13

said I could go to work on the night shift, one night or seven nights a week. I was large for my age and two summers of plowing with a team of mules on a farm in Tennessee had given me well-developed muscles. The shift began at eleven in the evening and ended at seven-thirty the next morning, and there was a half-hour lunch period from two-thirty to three. The pay was a dollar a night.

I knew that my mother, who before her marriage was Caroline Preston Bell, of Staunton, Virginia, and who had taught Latin and French at Chatham Hall, an Episcopal school for girls at Chatham, Virginia, was not going to consent to my working on the night shift in a cottonseed oil mill at the expense of my education and health. I decided it would be better if I did not say anything about it to my parents.

By going to bed early on the nights I planned to work, I hoped my parents would be led to believe I was getting a good night's sleep. Shortly before eleven o'clock I would dress and run a quarter of a mile to the mill, punch the time clock, and shovel cottonseed into conveyor troughs until morning. The cottonseed was carried in the troughs to another building where first it was hulled and then crushed in a powerful compress until the oil was extracted. The yellow cakes that remained were ground into meal and, together with the hulls, marketed for cattle feed.

There were usually ten or twelve laborers in the large cottonseed storage building, among them often being one or two high-school boys and nearly always three or four

Negroes. It seemed to me at the time, and I still believe it is true, that nothing of the smallest consequence took place in Wrens or in the nearby surrounding country that was not known in all its details to everyone of us at the mill. Family feuds, secreted births, mysterious deaths, violent quarrels, desertions, infidelities, and scandalous love-makings were freely and exhaustively discussed through the night by white and Negro alike. Working together in the seed house and eating early-morning lunch together on the railroad siding in fair weather and in the boiler room on rainy nights, there was no intimation of racial distinction, and everyone, white or Negro, was entitled to express his opinion and his likes and dislikes on any subject he wished. There may have been other such places, though I doubt it, but as far as I knew the cottonseed oil mill was the only completely democratic institution in town.

When daylight came in the morning, the gray dawn revealing the tired faces of men and boys shoveling cottonseed into conveyor troughs, it always seemed to me that all the momentous problems of twelve hundred human beings, as well as trifling and insignificant problems, had been thoroughly analyzed, catalogued, and disposed of. There would be new happenings and outright scandal to talk about when we came back to work that night.

The foreman had given me permission to punch the time clock half an hour before the end of the shift so I could go home and appear at breakfast at the regular time. At eight-twenty I went off to school for the day.

Call It Experience

I was able to stand this for almost two months, working from two to five nights a week, before sleep finally and completely overcame me, but by that time I had earned and saved almost thirty dollars. I was sure my mother had suspected that I was doing something I would not have been permitted to do, but nothing was said until I fell asleep at the breakfast table one morning. That was the end of my job at the cottonseed oil mill.

Summer vacation was soon to come, and my father, who I think was perhaps secretly proud, or even envious, of what I had done, let it be known that there would be no objections, if I wanted to continue working, to my finding a suitable daytime job in a store or shop. A few days before school closed for the summer I got a job turning the hand press at the plant of the local weekly newspaper, *The Jefferson Reporter*, edited and owned by Charlie Stephens. The following week I was given the additional task of setting type by hand, and a week after that I was told I could also collect social notes for the society page and write news items about happenings of interest. I took the money I had earned at the oil mill and bought a secondhand typewriter in Augusta. Charlie Stephens said he had no objection to my using my own typewriter on the job.

Evidently the newspaper prospered that summer, because during the hottest part of the season Charlie decided to take a vacation at Tybee Beach, near Savannah, and left me with the job of writing copy for the six-page sheet, setting the type by hand, printing the paper, folding, addressing, and delivering it to subscribers.

The circulation of the *Reporter* being approximately six hundred copies at that time, I found that I had a full-time job six days a week, even though two of the inside pages were boiler-plated. Charlie returned from the seashore in fine spirits at the end of two long weeks, tanned and healthy in appearance, and glanced through the issues I had got out during his absence. He seemed to be pleased with my work and said I was getting out a professional-looking paper. He also said I could keep on getting out the *Reporter* for a while longer. After calling on some of the merchants who owed him money for advertising, he went off fishing in a creek somewhere in Middle Georgia for a week.

By the time Charlie came back to town, I had got up enough courage to ask about my wages. I had figured that he owed me for seven weeks' work on *The Jefferson Reporter*. Charlie looked very surprised when I mentioned wages. I followed him across the pressroom and asked him a second time about my pay.

"You didn't expect me to pay you money for learning the business," he stated, shaking his head gravely.

I told him that I thought I should be paid something for the work I had done.

"Look here now, Erskine," he said. "You must have forgot you walked in here of your own free will and said you wanted to go to work for me. Not a single word was said about paying you for learning newspapering. You know that's true as well as I do."

"But I thought you'd want to pay me something, Mr. Stephens. They paid me a dollar a night when I shoveled cottonseed down at the oil mill. I've earned that much working for you, haven't I, Mr. Stephens?"

"Boy, you'd better hustle back down there to the mill and try to get your old job back, if money's all you're after in life."

"But couldn't you pay me even fifty cents a day, Mr. Stephens?" I asked him.

"No!" he said, shaking his head emphatically.

I thought about this during the next week, and then asked Charlie if he had any objection to my quitting the job. I was given to understand that I was not proving to be a loyal worker, but that since summer was almost over anyway, I could quit if I wanted to. I quit.

3.

My savings were now tied up in a secondhand typewriter and I had given up the only available job in town where I might have continued using it. I went to the ice plant and asked for work, but there was no job to be had. The two drugstores and the half a dozen or so grocery stores had all the help they needed. The cotton chopping season was over, and it was too early for picking cotton. I wished I had not given up my job on *The Jefferson Reporter*.

Finally, like almost every boy and man in Wrens that summer, I began going to the baseball games played several times a week between the local semi-pro club and teams from towns in nearby communities. The club manager had other worries, mostly financial, and readily agreed to let me keep the box score of the games played in Wrens. After a week or so I was able to do a fairly creditable job, and I was appointed, without salary, official scorer for the club. I was given a pass to all home games and permitted to sit on the players' bench, and sometimes I was allowed to take a road trip with the team to a nearby town.

While working at the *Reporter* I had made the discovery that most of the daily newspapers in the state employed local string correspondents. String correspondents, who were paid on the basis of two dollars a column for news items actually published, were expected to clip their printed dispatches, paste them into strings of column length, and mail them to the business manager of the paper at the end of each month. In my opinion little of state-wide interest that could be printed in a newspaper took place in Wrens in a year's time, certainly not a whole column monthly, and so I decided it would be more worthwhile, for my purposes, to approach the sports department of the nearest morning daily, *The Augusta Chronicle.*

The sports editor of the *Chronicle* promptly sent me a batch of self-addressed stamped envelopes in reply and I took this to mean that I had been officially appointed string correspondent for the *Chronicle* in Wrens. Whether the *Chronicle* actually had a considerable number of readers in Wrens, or whether the baseball games played that summer by the Wrens team were extraordinarily exciting to read about, I nevertheless found that the *Chronicle* was printing practically every word I wrote and mailed in. I was soon publishing, almost daily, column-length reports of games complete with box score and by-line.

My earnings as a string correspondent might have been larger if I had ignored the warning of the club manager after a particularly crucial game played in Wrens. He threatened to take away my pass and bar me from the baseball park if I sent in a column-length, blow-by-blow, bite-by-bite account that I had written of a savage fight between a visiting catcher and one of the local fans which ended with the ball player losing a portion of one of his ears and the fan being carried home unconscious. The manager claimed that such a story in the paper would hurt the gate receipts for the remainder of the season.

The end of the baseball season was a severe letdown. I returned to school that fall feeling that I was once more without a job and the means of earning money. I still had my typewriter, though, and I could now write with two fingers instead of with only one.

I wrote to the state news editors of all the daily papers in Georgia and offered my services as string correspondent in my locality. I received no reply from the Savannah papers, but I did receive without comment batches of self-addressed stamped envelopes from *The Atlanta Constitution* and *The Macon Telegraph*. During the following several months I sent to those newspapers, as well as to *The Augusta Chronicle*, complete reports of what I hoped would be considered important events that had taken place in our corner of Jefferson County. The published results were disappointing, and in no manner comparable in length to the printed accounts of baseball games played in Wrens the past summer. Somebody connected with each newspaper was systematically chopping my one- and two-page news dispatches down to measly two- or three-inch items. It took a long time to paste up a twenty-two-inch column.

Hoping to better myself, I went over to the competition. I dropped the *Constitution* for the *Journal* in Atlanta; I switched from the *Telegraph* to the *News* in Macon; and in Augusta I changed from the *Chronicle* to the *Herald*. This scheme did not work out so well. My strings were even shorter at the end of the month. I then realized that the morning dailies had more circulation in Wrens than the afternoon papers, the reason being that the former were delivered the day of publication. Afternoon papers sometimes did not arrive until the following day. I went back to corresponding for morning papers.

Still searching for a way to increase the length of my pasted-up columns, I asked my father the following spring to take me to call on the various state news editors. He agreed to take me to Macon and we made the hundred-mile trip over dusty unpaved roads in our eight-year-old Ford. Leaving home at six o'clock in the morning, and after a number of punctures and blowouts, as well as having to stop several times to clean the spark plugs, we reached Macon about two o'clock in the afternoon. I had no idea what I was going to say to the news editor when we reached Macon, and by the time we entered the office of the *Telegraph*, I wished I had never thought of attempting such a thing.

Call It Experience

The news editor of *The Macon Telegraph* was Mark Ethridge. He was the first authentic newspaperman I had ever seen at work, and I was too awed by the situation to do much more than nod my head several times when I was spoken to. My father and Mark sat and talked, almost exclusively about Georgia politics, for at least an hour. In the end, just as we were shaking hands and getting ready to leave, my father spoke up for me. He remarked that I had been sending the *Telegraph* correspondence from Wrens for several months.

Mark said he had read some of the items I had mailed to the paper. Then with a smile he said the business office considered Wrens outside the *Telegraph's* primary circulation territory, probably even outside the secondary circulation territory, and that it was doubtful if the paper had as many as a dozen subscribers in all of Jefferson County.

I do not know what prompted me to suggest it, though no doubt because I wanted to maintain some connection with a newspaper, but I offered to sell the *Telegraph* in Wrens if I were given a job as newsboy. I had sold papers on the street in Charlotte and Staunton when I was much younger.

Laughing, Mark shook his head. "You don't really want to peddle papers, now do you, Erskine?" he asked.

"I'd rather write for them," I said at once.

"I thought so," he said seriously. "You've been trying hard to get something into the *Telegraph*. I'll tell you what you can do. Go back to Wrens and write about things you see happening. Don't take anybody's word for anything. See it yourself, or don't believe it. There's always something to write about sooner or later in any town. And if you can make it interesting enough, it'll get printed. Don't worry about that. It's all in the way you see it and write about it that's going to count. Good luck!"

After leaving Mark Ethridge, we went down to Cherry Street and stopped at a lunchroom and ate baked ham and sweet potatoes and apple pie. I was just as hungry as ever when the meal was finished, and my father bought a dozen cinnamon rolls for us to eat during the long dusty trip home. I remember the day very clearly, because every time my father bought cinnamon rolls for us to eat he always called them sugar-babes.

4.

Early in the summer of 1919 I began taking day-long automobile trips into the country with one of the local physicians whose patients were scattered for miles along creeks and on hillsides over portions of Jefferson, Burke, and Glascock Counties. I received no pay for driving the car and making minor repairs, and expected none; I was interested only in seeing how people lived in the country and I was glad to have such an opportunity. Sometimes the doctor would have been up all night, and he would sleep soundly during the time it took me to patch an inner tube or drive from the home of one patient to the next. He made no distinction between those who were able to pay for his services and those who were not, and often he provided the necessary medicine as well. Sometimes, where hardship was extreme, I saw him leave a dollar or two on a chair or table.

Later I began going on trips into the country with the county tax assessor as he nimbly combined political fence-mending with adjustment of assessments. I soon learned to be able to foretell with some accuracy whether we would be invited into a farmer's home for a noon-time meal. If the farmer felt that his tax adjustment had been sufficiently favorable and failed to argue too much about it, I could be fairly certain that we would be urged to stay for dinner. Otherwise, while the tax assessor mumbled profanely about the stinginess of some people in this world, we drove to the nearest crossroad store and ate daisy cheese and soda crackers.

At other times that summer my father took me with him when he visited members of his church in the country. However, church members were not the only ones visited; more frequently he called at the home of a non-churchgoer.

In almost every instance there seemed to be a common pattern of life at that time in this tenant-farming cotton country. Tobacco had been raised in large quantities in this same sand-clay soil many years before, and a few abandoned tobacco roads—broad flat trails made by heavy hogsheads of cured tobacco being rolled from farms to the Savannah River—were still to be seen on the crests of several of the blackjack ridges. Most of the landowners lived in comparative comfort in the nearby towns of Waynesboro, Louisville, and Wrens, while in the country itself there was poverty on all sides, the only apparent variation being in the degree of it.

Sometimes there were signs and evidences of more dire want than my father could look upon without comment. He would stop the car beside the weed-bordered road and gaze back over the cotton fields at the one- or two-room dilapidated frame tenant house we had just left. Most of the shingle-rotted shacks contained a bed and several pallets on the floor, a cook-stove, and a few split-cane straight-back chairs.

"That poor chap back there hasn't got a chance in the world to get out of the rut he's in as long as he lives," my father would say sadly. "He's as bad off as a toad in a post hole. It's a disgrace that human beings have to live like that. And all those children. What's to become of them when they grow up? Be toads in post holes, too?"

There was no answer to that, because neither of us knew the answer. After a while we would drive on down the gully-washed dirt road in silence in the afternoon heat to the next tenant family we were going to visit.

We ourselves were not considered wealthy, or even well-to-do, but most of the people I saw were existing on a far lower economic level. My father's salary as a minister had been four hundred dollars annually when he first came from the theological seminary and, even when he taught school to augment his income, he never received more than two thousand dollars a year during his lifetime.

However, there was a helpful custom in the church for many years that provided the minister's family with periodic aid in the form of farm produce.

The practice, called pounding, was for the more affluent members of the congregation to bring one pound or several pounds of meat, flour, sugar, and other staple food to the parsonage several times a year. We were never hungry, but often I did not have just what I would have liked to have to eat. There was no doubt, though, that many persons around us were hungry year after year. I do not remember a single occasion when my father was not asked for food during our trips into the country. He made it a habit, even when my mother said there was none too much for the three of us, always to carry a sack of potatoes or flour and a bag of grits or black-eyed peas in the car with him wherever he went. My mother more often than not added a small bag of candy for the old people and children.

5.

In September, three months before my seventeenth birthday, I went away to college. I was sorry to put aside my ambition to write acceptable news correspondence for the papers in Macon and Augusta, but I was beginning to feel confined by the limited horizons of East Georgia and I wanted to know more of the world beyond.

I had attended high school for only two years, both of them in Wrens, and did not have sufficient credits to graduate. Beyond that my formal education had been obtained during two years of grammar-school attendance in Tennessee and a portion of a year in a private school at Fairfield, Rockbridge County, Virginia.

I entered the freshman class at Erskine College, Due West, South Carolina, an institution maintained by the Associate Reformed Presbyterian church. My father had graduated there, from both the college and the theological seminary, and the expenses were so little that he felt he could afford to borrow the money to send me. It was my first experience of being away from home. I liked the comparative freedom of college life, but I was made unhappy by the prospect of having to devote so much time solely to education within the relatively small area of the campus. After several weeks of restlessness I got into the habit of spending week ends elsewhere whenever I could. I found that the least costly means of getting from Due West to some other place was to climb aboard a freight train Friday or Saturday night and to go as far as the train would take me by morning. I usually went to Greenville, Spartanburg, Anderson, Greenwood, or Columbia, and returned to Due West on a freight train Sunday night or early Monday morning.

Being a freshman, certain rules and regulations were prescribed for me by upperclassmen. There were three such orders that left the deepest impression upon me. I was told to make the freshman football team or suffer harsh consequences; to smuggle complete meals three times a day from the dining hall for a poker game that ran almost without interruption from the opening of school to the Christmas holidays and from the re-opening in January to commencement in June; and, finally, to seek out, invite, and produce in person a comely out-of-town young woman between the ages of seventeen and twenty for every scheduled athletic event on the campus.

I liked playing football, I did not mind carrying food to the poker players, and, since it had been made clear that a different young woman had to be invited each time, I did meet a considerable number of South Carolina young women that year. However, with three standing duties to perform, I found little opportunity for study. My grades at the end of my freshman year were so low that even I was surprised. I was given to understand by the authorities that I would be permitted to return for my sophomore year only if I would agree to subscribe in full to certain scholastic requirements.

When the college term was over the first of June, I went to Calhoun, Georgia, a small town in the Blue Ridge Piedmont fifty miles from Chattanooga, Tennessee, where I got a job as a stonemason's helper. There were only the two of us working on the project, which was the construction of a granite-block church, and I soon found out that I had the hardest job I had ever undertaken. At the end of summer, though, when the granite walls had been erected to roof level, I was in good physical condition for football, and I went back to Erskine College and made the varsity team the first week of practice.

When the football season closed in November, I was restless without the strenuous physical activity I had become accustomed to during the summer and fall. Shortly after returning to school from the Christmas holidays I decided to get out into the world. I chose New Orleans as the place to go, both because I had never been there and because I had saved enough money to take me that far away.

After eating less and less each succeeding day for nearly two weeks, and failing to sign aboard a Gulf of Mexico freighter as a deck hand, I went to Bogalusa, Louisiana, in search of a job. The town was on the Pearl River seventy-five miles north of New Orleans and was the location of a large lumber mill. Bogalusa was also the scene of labor difficulty at the time, and a large billboard at the railroad station notified I.W.W.'s and other labor agitators to go elsewhere or suffer the penalty of arrest.

This public warning meant nothing to me and I was certain I would be able to get work in Bogalusa. I was at the employment gate of the lumber mill at six o'clock every morning for a week, and losing weight rapidly. At the end of the football season I had weighed a hundred and seventy-seven pounds, and I was down to a hundred and thirty-four. Even if I had been given a job in the mill, I probably would not have lasted a full shift peeling logs.

I did not know why, although I thought probably one reason was because I had been unable to pay my room rent for the past week, but I found myself being escorted from the rooming house by two untalkative plainclothesmen. Within the space of a few minutes' time I was stating my name and age to somebody seated at a scarred booking desk and then I was in one of the ceiling-high cells of the city jail. Afterward, when I had plenty of time to think about what had happened, I remembered that the police officer at the booking desk had muttered a brief remark about the International Workers of the World signing up junior members before they were much out of knee-pants.

I was provided with food twice a day by a middle-aged Negro trusty who shoved a pail of soggy turnip greens and fat-back through the bars without comment. Every time he passed by, I called to the trusty and asked if he knew why I was being kept there.

"You'd better ask the white folks, boss," the Negro answered hurriedly each time. "I done been told I don't know nothing. I sure know how you feel, though, because I feel like I've been locked up in here all my life my own self."

It was useless to try to get the attention of anyone in the front room of the jail in order to ask why I had been locked up and when I would be released; the jailer had a habit of slamming shut the steel firedoor when anybody in the cellroom annoyed him.

After three days and nights I was beginning to think I would never get out. A boy of twenty in the cell next to mine gave me an envelope, I got a pencil and a sheet of paper from somebody else, and I wrote a letter to my father telling him where I was and how much I would like to get out and come home. I had five cents in my pocket for a stamp, but I was advised not to give it to the jailer if I expected the letter to be mailed. The Negro trusty was afraid to have anything to do with it. Climbing to the top of the cell and hanging to the bars over the one small window, I waited for somebody to pass by on the outside.

There was no street on that side of the jail, only a weed-grown vacant lot, and it was not often during the day that anyone came that way. Just before dusk I saw a small Negro boy playing on the far side of the lot. I called several times before he would venture close to the jail. The boy, who looked to be about eight or nine years old, was suspicious of anybody who would call to him from the jail window, and I had to convince him that he would not get into trouble merely by listening to what I wanted to ask him. He finally promised faithfully to buy a stamp and mail the letter for me. I gave him the nickel, telling him the change was his to keep, and also my silver-plated college belt-buckle. The boy ran off into the darkness after that. I lay awake all night silently praying that the letter would be mailed.

On the fourth day following, just at nightfall, a tall young man who said he was the Y.M.C.A. secretary in Bogalusa came into the cellroom with the jailer and told me that I was going to be released at once. In a few minutes we were riding in a car to the Y.M.C.A. building. There was a meal on the table and the secretary had got together some clean clothes for me to wear. After a steamy hot shower I put on the clean clothes and ate every morsel of food.

While I was eating, the secretary told me that my father had received my letter and telegraphed money for my train fare home. He said further that a train would be leaving for Birmingham in about forty-five minutes. I was the first passenger to board the train when it arrived at the station. The last thing I remembered seeing in Bogalusa was the brightly illuminated billboard with its pertinent warning.

I arrived home late the next afternoon. My father was at the depot when I got off the train from Atlanta. He came up and shook hands with me and smiled without a trace of displeasure. I was glad to see him, too.

I can recall only one thing that was said as we walked along the sandy tree-shaded street toward our house.

"What did you think of Louisiana, son?" my father asked. "It's nothing like this part of the country, is it?"

6.

In April I got my typewriter from the closet and began sending news items to the morning papers in Macon, Augusta, and Atlanta. I liked being a string correspondent as much as ever, and I found that my dispatches concerning births, deaths, and accidents were published more frequently and in greater length than in previous years, but I soon realized that I missed college life and I wanted to return to it.

It was understood without discussion that my parents could not afford the expense of sending me to Georgia Tech or the University of Georgia. However, I knew I would not be satisfied with anything less than the opportunities offered by a large university, and I began looking for ways and means of getting what I wanted. After a study of a large number of catalogues and bulletins, and with the encouragement of my mother, I decided upon the University of Virginia.

It was quite a shock to learn that the yearly tuition fee charged non-Virginians amounted to several hundred dollars. The least expensive room and board I could obtain in Charlottesville was twice as much as I had paid in Due West. Including tuition, and figuring other expenses closely, the cost of attending the University of Virginia amounted to at least twelve hundred dollars a year. My father said he could let me have a third of the sum.

My academic record discouraged me from applying for a scholastic scholarship at Virginia. But I discovered that there was a different type of scholarship available, and that the required qualifications had little to do with grades and units. This was a scholarship that provided the full amount of tuition and it was offered by a chapter of the United Daughters of the Confederacy to a student who was a resident of Georgia. The Civil War had been over a long time, and the scholarship evidently had not been granted for many years, but I had no hesitancy about reviving the subject. The important requirement was that the applicant must prove that, maternally or paternally, he was a descendent of a soldier in the Confederate Army who had taken part in the War Between the States. I think the United Daughters of the Confederacy must have been surprised to learn that the scholarship was still being offered, but I was able to qualify, and the scholarship was granted to me.

Call It Experience

I entered the University of Virginia in September, 1922. Within a short time I had a job, the hours being from six p.m. to midnight, six nights a week, working as clerk-cashier-janitor in a pool hall near the campus. The salary of six dollars a week which I received, together with the money supplied by my parents, enabled me to pay for my room, board, textbooks, and clothing.

The subjects that interested me most at Virginia were English and sociology. After field trips to state hospitals and county old-age homes and similar institutions, I began writing about what I had seen. At first I wrote strictly factual reports, much like the newspaper correspondence I had done, but gradually I began using the same material as the inspiration for sketches and brief stories. Soon I was more interested in writing my impressions than I was in composing theme papers on such English course assignments as "What Wordsworth Means to Me" and "Humanity as Exemplified by the Lake Poets."

Writing became such an absorbing interest that I began experimenting with many forms of it. I began submitting jokes, mostly of the he-and-she variety, to *The Virginia Reel*, the university humor magazine. Edward R. Stettinius, Jr., who was on the editorial board of the magazine, spent considerable time arguing about what constituted college humor. Probably because Arthur Hawkins was drawing for *The Virginia Reel*, he maintained that comic drawings should take up more than half the space in the *Reel*. Ed was on the editorial board and I was not, and the publication continued to appear with nearly twice as much space devoted to art work as went to literary content. The jokes that I could not get into the *Reel* were submitted to, and some were published in, humorous magazines with national circulation. The pay I received was usually a dollar for each joke published.

Several students at the university were writing books, but I hesitated to make the attempt. Charles Wertenbaker wrote a novel, and James Aswell wrote a book of poems. Gordon Lewis, who owned a bookshop near the campus, encouraged me by saying he would publish any book I wrote if, in his opinion, it had extraordinary merit and promising sales prospects.

In my desire to learn to write fiction, and to get it published by Gordon Lewis or by anyone else, I frequently changed courses and even dropped out of the university for long intervals while searching for the way to write. I knew how I wanted to write and what I wanted to write about. I wanted to write about the people I knew as they really lived, moved, and talked. During the four years that I was an in-and-out student at Virginia, only two years of which were actually spent in residence, I worked a milk delivery route for a while in Washington, D.C., spent several months working behind the counter in an orange drink stand in Philadelphia, and was for four months a stock clerk in charge of crockery and glassware in the basement of a variety store in Wilkes-Barre, Pennsylvania.

Finally, in the spring of 1925, I felt that I could wait no longer to start doing in earnest whatever I was going to do in life. Twenty-one years old, and still two years short of graduation, I left Charlottesville and went to Georgia and applied for a job on *The Atlanta Journal*. I had no ambition to make journalism my lifework, but newspaper work was writing, and that was what I wanted to learn to do.

Hunter Bell, the *Journal* city editor, was not enthusiastic about employing anybody fresh from college, but he agreed to take me on as a cub reporter, on a trial basis, at a salary of twenty dollars a week.

I thanked Hunter gratefully for giving me a job and told him that I would be back in three or four days to go to work. I was halfway across the city room when he recovered enough to yell at me.

"Hey! Come back here!" he shouted. "What's this about coming to work three or four days from now?"

I told him I wanted to go back to Charlottesville to pack up my things and bring them to Atlanta.

"What things?" he asked interestedly.

"Well, I've got some books, and a few other—"

"Books! If I'd known you think more of some bologna-stuffed books than you do about a newspaper job, I'd never have hired you. I think I'll take that job back, anyway. I want a reporter—not a bookworm!"

"All right, Mr. Bell," I said meekly, "I'll stay and go to work right away."

"Yeh. That's more like it, Caldwell. Now find yourself a typewriter and call up all the undertakers in town and get some obits."

7.

There was much to learn, and unlearn as well, about the writing of a simple news story. First of all I had to put aside the wordy way of writing I had got into while working as a string correspondent several years before, and then I had to acquire the skill to write what Hunter Bell considered a readable news item.

The city editor would begin his copy reading by whisking a soft-lead pencil over a three- or four-hundred-word story about a fire or a holdup or an accident until there were perhaps a dozen lines left, and then he would hand it back to me and say he could use it only if I rewrote the story in half as many lines. This was a realistic course of instruction in writing, completely different from anything I had learned in English courses anywhere, and from that time forward I was glad something had prompted me to go to work on a newspaper.

One of my first news assignments on *The Atlanta Journal*—other than phoning the local mortuaries and writing a column of obituaries, which I did every morning for a year—was to go to an address in downtown Atlanta near Five Points and find out how a man had come to die in a dollar-a-night walk-up hotel.

When I got to the address on Marietta Street, the police were there making an investigation. The only information the police had was the name the dead man had scrawled on the hotel register the night before, but the police decided the name he had used was a fictitious one. The body of the supposedly itinerant laborer, who had been shot once through the head with a small rusty pistol, was ordered removed to the city morgue and the case was closed.

After the police had left, I asked the hotel clerk if he knew any reason why the man had committed suicide. The clerk had a very definite idea.

"It's Monday morning, ain't it?" he said. "Well, what do you figure always happens on blue Monday? I'll tell you. That fellow they carried out of here felt just like all the other poor devils who've waked up stony-broke Monday morning after throwing away last week's pay, and he decided he'd had a bellyful of it. That's blue Monday, friend. And believe me, that's when they pull out that little old gun and blast themselves to kingdom-come."

I asked him if it had ever happened in the hotel before.

"Has it! I've been here two years now, and it happens too often to suit me. Sometimes I hate to wake up Monday morning myself, because I can't get used to seeing what blue Monday will do to somebody in that fix. One of these days I'm going to pick up and go back to South Georgia where the folks don't know what blue Monday is."

I went back to my desk at the *Journal* and began writing about a discouraged, penniless, middle-aged man who felt that life had treated him badly and as a result had lost all desire to continue an existence in an unfeeling, unsympathetic, hard-hearted world. After two hours or more I had written several pages, and at noon Hunter left his desk to go out to lunch. On his way out, he stopped and read the sheet in my typewriter. When he finished, he lit a cigar.

"Maybe you don't know it, Erskine, but the noon edition's on the street now," he said. "The final will be out in a few hours. It'd be a shame to have to hold up the presses and replate page one for that story I sent you out to get at nine o'clock this morning. I'd sort of counted on getting away on time this afternoon and going out to Grant Park and paddle around in a boat for a while. That's about the only fun I get out of life and I'd sure hate to miss it."

I tried to explain that I needed all that time to write the story about the man who had killed himself in the hotel.

"It's a big story, Hunter. This fellow shot himself because it was blue Monday."

"Yeh? What are you doing—writing his five-dollar-a-copy biography?"

"But this is really a good story, Hunter. Just think—here was an ordinary man, just like you and me, who woke up this morning and killed himself just because it was blue Monday."

"Yeh?" Hunter said, nodding slowly. "What color do you think Tuesday would be for me if the managing editor fired me for not putting this sheet on the street on schedule—just because I held it up waiting for you to polish up a story?"

Call It Experience

He picked up the phone and talked to police head-quarters. After a minute or so he put the phone down. "No name. No home address. No story." He jerked the sheet of paper out of my typewriter and threw it into the wastebasket. "Now give me half a stick for the final about the police finding the body of an unidentified man in a room on Marietta Street this morning. That's ·all. When I want a sob story, I'll send Peggy Mitchell."

Margaret Mitchell was a feature writer at that time on the staff of the *Journal's* Sunday magazine and her desk was on another floor of the building. Hunter used various means to try to persuade Peggy to write special stories for him and, although he rarely succeeded, he refused to stop trying, because he considered Peggy to be the best writer of human-interest stories on the paper. Frank Daniel, a reporter whose desk was next to mine, told me that Peggy was going to resign and leave newspaper work to write a novel she had planned for many years. Hunter refused to believe it until she did not come to work one morning. All he would say then was that writing books was a fly-by-night occupation and he hoped nobody else on the *Journal* would ever make the same mistake.

Even if Peggy had not had a striking personality and an engaging way of talking, besides being unusually attractive, I still would have been impressed by her. I admired her for having enough confidence in herself to give up her job to write a book, and I wondered if I would ever be able to make a similar decision. I said nothing to Hunter about my ambition to write books, because I knew what his reaction would be, but nevertheless I was thinking about it more and more all the time. Anyway, Peggy Mitchell had resigned and, after ten years of work, *Gone With the Wind* was published in 1936.

It was during this time, the fall and winter of 1925–26, that I had the opportunity to observe, though not exactly at close hand, the day-to-day progress of an author actively engaged in the profession of fiction writing. I had been deeply impressed by a book, *The Short Story's Mutations*, that Frances Newman had edited the year before, and now almost every day Frank Daniel, who was a close friend of hers, brought to the *Journal* city room, over a period of several months, a typescript page of the novel Frances was working on. Each page was a complete day's work on *The Hard-Boiled Virgin*. The finished page, so neatly typed and without corrections, always looked as if it had been written with ease and without laborious revision, but Frank assured me that it was the final result of a full day's rewriting.

I would go home in the evening and write short stories and mail them to magazine editors in New York. The stories, no matter how many times I rewrote them, were always returned, usually without comment, with unfailing promptness. I received so many rejection slips, and such an interesting variety, that I began making a collection of them, keeping them pasted neatly in a stamp collector's album. The only consolation I ever got out of them for many years was in visualizing how big a bonfire I could make with them when I had my first short story accepted and published in a magazine.

8.

Before the end of 1925 I wrote to a number of newspapers in Alabama, Georgia, and the Carolinas saying I would like to write reviews for their book sections. Only one reply was received. This was a prompt, enthusiastic letter from Cora Harris, the editor of the Sunday book page of *The Charlotte Observer*.

Cora said she had been looking for somebody to help her with reviews for a long time, that she would be delighted to send me some books for review, and in fact was mailing half a dozen that same day. She expressed regret that she would not be able to offer payment for the reviews, but added, however, that I could keep the books.

I was having trouble holding on to enough of my salary to pay the rent, among other things, and I had hoped to be able to earn a few dollars a week in addition to my salary of twenty dollars. Frank Daniel told me that I would probably be able to sell any of the review copies I did not wish to keep, and I agreed to contribute reviews to the *Observer*. Within a short time I was writing notices of a dozen or more books a week, and I found that the more reviews I wrote, and the quicker I mailed them to Charlotte, the more books I received. I sold a few of the mystery stories and some of the esoteric novels at a secondhand bookshop on Forsyth Street, usually for a quarter each, but kept the greater portion of them. At the end of three or four months I had several hundred volumes of novels, poetry, biography, anthologies, and how-to books on practically all conceivable subjects.

It was pleasing to receive, early in 1926, a letter from Cora Harris informing me that the reviews I was writing were now appearing each Sunday in *The Houston Post,* in addition to *The Charlotte Observer,* and saying that I could look forward to receiving even more books for review in the future. I felt sure now that the reviews were being syndicated that I would begin receiving some payment any day. Soon books began arriving from Charlotte by the score several times a week. My room was stacked to the ceiling with them. Still looking forward hopefully to the day when I would receive at least token payment for my reviews, I read more rapidly than ever or looked more closely at the jacket of the book, and wrote briefer notices. But still no payment came.

Writing as many reviews as I was doing, an additional two or three was no strain, and I began contributing to the *Journal's* Sunday book-review page. I was paid two dollars each for the reviews printed in the *Journal.*

After six months on the *Journal* I was given a five-dollar-a-week raise in salary by Hunter Bell and initiated into the local brotherhood of reporters. The salary now amounted to twenty-five dollars weekly. The initiation was a nightmare involving a fictitious uprising of enlisted men against authority at Fort McPherson, an army base near Atlanta, and the equally fictitious fatal shooting of a number of innocent bystanders, among whom were said to be the governor of Georgia, the mayor of Atlanta, the batboy of the Atlanta baseball club, a visiting Hollywood movie actress, Bobby Jones, and Fuzzy Woodruff. All this originated at a downstairs switchboard with a group of sports-department reporters interrupting their on-the-spot reports by *rat-tat-tatting* with a pencil on the mouthpiece of the telephone.

By two o'clock in the morning I had the entire front page of the Sunday final edition remade, complete with a list of known dead, eyewitness reports by hysterical East Point housewives, and statements from the ministerial association and the chamber of commerce deploring the tragic event. It was not until the sports-department reporters became tired and called an end to the hoax at three o'clock that I found out that I had undergone initiation.

When I arrived for work Monday morning, Hunter Bell, without a comment concerning the Saturday-night initiation, said he wanted me to hurry down to the Kimball House, a nearby hotel, and cover an eclectic convention.

I asked Hunter if he meant an electric convention.

"You ought to know what eclectics are, Erskine," he said without looking up from the copy he was reading. "Those people are doctors, not electricians."

Hunter still had not looked me straight in the face and by that time I was certain he was attempting to prolong the initiation. I was determined not to be fooled again by a fake story.

On the way to the Kimball House I stopped at a restaurant and ate a leisurely second breakfast, had my shoes shined, and watched a steam shovel excavating for the foundation of a new building. An hour or so later I strolled into the Kimball House and sat down in the rear of the convention hall. I watched the proceedings from a distance for about half an hour and decided, since no talks had been made, that committee conferences were being held.

Most of the men present were seated in small groups laughing and joking. They were conservatively dressed elderly men. They looked to me as much like presidents of utility companies as anything else, and by that time I was confident they were.

About two hours after lunch I phoned Hunter and told him that one of the men at the convention had invented a new electric-light bulb, said to be the greatest scientific advance in the field since Thomas A. Edison, and asked how much of a story he wanted on it. I told him not to forget to send a photographer to get a picture of the new bulb.

When I finished talking, there was a long silence before I heard Hunter's voice.

"Where are you now, Erskine?" he asked finally.

"At the Kimball House."

"Have you been at that convention all day?"

I told him I had been in and out since I got there that morning.

"In and out of what?" he demanded unpleasantly.

"The electric convention," I told him.

"Then what about that convention of eclectic doctors I sent you to cover!"

45

I began to worry.

"Hunter, do you think these people are really doctors?" I asked.

"I know so. What've you been doing down there all day?"

"Getting the story," I said quickly. "Don't worry, Hunter! I'll have it for you, even if it takes me all night. You don't have to wait for me, either. Go on out to Grant Park and paddle around in your boat. I'm going to take care of this."

I put down the phone and hastily found several convention delegates. Every single one of them readily admitted being an eclectic physician. After talking to them, I went back to the city room and wrote a half-column story about the progress of eclecticism in the United States and its effect on human life.

After reading my story in the early edition the next morning, the managing editor gave Hunter a handful of cigars and complimented him for running the only story about eclectic physicians that he had ever been able to understand during his long career in the newspaper business.

9.

In the midyear of 1926 I decided my next step should be to give up my job and leave Atlanta. I had worked on the *Journal* for a year, I had written perhaps forty or fifty short stories, not one of which had been published, and

Call It Experience

I had about two thousand volumes of fiction and non-fiction I had been given in lieu of pay for reviewing. Besides, I had finally saved almost two hundred dollars.

Of more importance to me, however, was the fact that during those past twelve months I had been coming to the realization that I wanted to be above all else a professional author. And as I saw it, there was only one authentic kind of writer—a writer who could see his stories in print. I have no recollection of the period when this decision became so firmly embedded in my consciousness that it grew to be a part of me, but I never for a moment afterward doubted its ability, or its willingness, to sustain me.

All wisdom and human experience aside, I was going to quit my job and devote full and exclusive time to the writing of short stories and novels. I promised myself that any occupation, other than writing, that I engaged in would be temporary and solely for the purpose of staying alive, keeping a roof over my head, and being adequately clothed. I put aside the next five years in which to accomplish my ambition, with the reservation that I would take an additional five years if necessary. I had no idea how I would support myself and fulfill personal obligations until I could learn to write fiction that editors would pay for, but that did not seem important at the time. I was confident that I would find a way when the need came.

After coming to the decision, and after making up my mind not to let anyone talk me into changing it, I then set out to choose some place in which to live. Except for several months spent in Pennsylvania, I had lived all my life in the South, and I wanted to be where I would find a new and different perspective. I intended to write about Southern life as I knew it and it seemed to me that I could best view it from a distance. Going abroad did not appeal to me; I wanted to live somewhere in the United States. In addition to the promise of inexpensive living costs, the State of Maine seemed to be a faraway place on the map. I decided to go Down East.

I began packing my books in wooden boxes for shipment by freight. I did not know what I was going to do with nearly two thousand review copies, especially since I had already read the ones that interested me, but they represented my only material possessions and were too valuable to give away or sell cheaply.

Frank Daniel, even if he had misgivings, gave no indications that he thought I was taking a misguided and fool-hardy step. He even went so far as to say that if he thought he had the ability to write fiction successfully, he hoped he would have the courage to do what I was about to undertake. He had already made up his mind to continue his newspaper career.

On the other hand, Hunter Bell tried to forewarn me of what I could expect if I insisted upon going recklessly ahead. He described a miserable future for those unfortunates in life who expected to live, eat, and walk the earth without the security of a job. After I had given two weeks' notice, Hunter still tried to get me to change my mind. He gave me several assignments seemingly calculated to show what I would miss if I left the paper.

One of the final assignments I had on the *Journal* was that of preparing for the Sunday edition a special section devoted to a year's review of the progress and accomplishments of the Atlanta Convention and Tourist Bureau, a non-profit organization supported by interested groups of businessmen. The secretary-manager of the bureau was Fred Houser, a good-mixer and jolly greeter who was given credit for bringing a number of large conventions to Atlanta each year.

On Monday morning following the appearance of the special section, which contained among other features a strikingly handsome photograph of the secretary-manager, Fred Houser came to the *Journal* city room. Hunter sent a copy boy for me.

Fred was beaming when I got to the city desk.

"I want to take you to lunch, Caldwell," Fred said, enthusiastically shaking my hand. "Wow! What a spread! A whole section, too! And pictures all over the thing!" He slapped me on the back several times. "That's the best story I ever had, Caldwell. People didn't know we had such a wonderful convention city right here in Atlanta until they read your write-up yesterday. That'll prove to businessmen what their support of the Convention and Tourist Bureau does for their bank balances. I've had calls already this morning from hard-fisted businessmen who want to ride on our train now. I'm going to cram the hotels so full of conventioneers this year that you'll see 'em sleeping with their feet hanging out the windows of the Ansley and the Piedmont. Let's go to the Rathskeller for lunch, Caldwell! My guest, of course! Order anything you want—pay no attention to the cost!"

Call It Experience

I thanked Fred and told him that I would meet him in the Ansley Hotel lobby at noon.

After Fred had gone, Hunter came over and sat down on the top of my desk.

"See there, Erskine?" he said earnestly. "That shows you what you can do around here. That's newspapering. It makes life worthwhile, doesn't it? You're too smart to want to take a chance writing books. Everybody knows it's a fly-by-night thing. Broke most of the time, and friends afraid to trust you for a few dollars until pay day. Even the loan-sharks are scared of it. If you stay here on the *Journal*, you know I'll give you a chit to the cashier for an advance against a week's salary anytime you need it." He stopped talking for a moment and watched me closely. "Now, do you still want to throw it all away?"

I told him I did.

He puffed on his cigar for a while, at the same time rolling it over and over in his mouth with his fingers. He continued to look directly at me, his expression unchanged.

"Yeh?" he said after several moments. "Well, so long, Erskine. Hope you don't have it too hard from now on, but you can always count on me to feel sorry for you."

Hunter then got up and walked away.

At the end of the week, I left Atlanta for the State of Maine.

10.

In early summer inland Maine, deep in silent damp forests, was an enchanting world of softly unfolding shades of green. The gently undulating hills were dark green islands of spruce and fir, the lush meadows bordering the meandering streams were verdant carpets, and the placid water of the lakes endlessly blue-green. The everlasting countryside was serene and unhurried, and the aches and pains of civilization were distantly remote. One could surely write in such a place, it seemed to say, if writing ever was to be done.

Summertime in Maine, though, I was soon to learn, was a brief season of a few weeks providentially granted mankind each year for the one purpose of husbanding for winter. That was the time to seek and acquire at any cost, for nine months of cold, the essential creature comforts of fuel and food.

Food meant potatoes, and I planted potatoes. Fuel meant wood, and I cut wood. Woodcutting soon became my daytime occupation. Writing short stories became a nighttime occupation, as did reviewing book after book for Cora Harris. And sleep, for a few month as least, became an almost unattainable luxury.

I had little conception of the quantity of wood needed to heat a large house from September to May. The century-old dwelling previously had been remodeled for use as a summer residence and had not been occupied in winter for many years. The house was ideally cool and airy in summer, a delight to vacationists and tourists, but it was viewed askance by natives who knew the discomfort of the subzero cold of midwinter nights. The gabled clapboard building of many rooms was situated on a moderate hill between two lakes in the Town of Mount Vernon, Kennebec County, and was exposed on three sides to the sweeping snow of a Maine winter. Of its many rooms, only two had stoves.

I asked my next-door neighbor, a farmer named Arthur Dolloff, who lived half a mile away, how many cords of wood did he think I would need for the winter. Arthur was a lifetime resident of Maine and had constructed his five-room, story-and-a-half saltbox house with native foresight. The walls and attic of his house were insulated, the rooms were small and low-ceilinged, and he kept the outside foundation banked in winter with sawdust and fir boughs for protection against the ground frost. His woodshed, the largest room in the house, was stacked the year around with well-seasoned hardwood.

Arthur carefully considered the proportions of the large rambling summer house on the hill before committing himself.

"Maybe eighteen-twenty cords," he estimated, cautiously adding, "that is, unless the Old Boy has a mind to give us a cold winter. Then I should want six-seven more for tolerable comfort."

"How cold does a cold winter get, Arthur?" I asked him.

"Twenty below nights, average."

I asked him if it stayed that cold for long at a time.

"Wouldn't be one to speculate against it, in the State of Maine, in my right mind."

"How long do you think it would take me to cut twenty cords and store it in the woodshed?"

"Not having the benefit of outside assistance?"

I told him I would be doing it alone.

"Guess from now to Groundhog Day, maybe a mite longer, weather depending."

"Then maybe I ought to get started right away," I said.

"Wouldn't doubt the wisdom of it," Arthur agreed. "Frostbite is a villainous thing."

It was the Fourth of July when I began cutting down birch trees in the woodlot and sawing the logs stove-length. White birch grew much closer to the house than the hardwood, and, since the sawn wood had to be dragged, carried, or rolled about two hundred yards to the woodshed, I cut no maple or beech. When the first snow fell not long after Labor Day, I had about ten cords of unseasoned white birch cut and stored. It looked like a great amount of wood to me and I was proud of what I had accomplished since I had been in Mount Vernon. I stopped cutting then; after all, we had only two stoves in the house.

When Arthur Dolloff saw the sap-damp unseasoned birch in the woodshed, he shook his head to himself.

"Cussed birch won't heat when it's green and won't last when it's dry," he commented. "Maybe next year you'll have a mind to cut rock maple and keep warm."

By the beginning of January most of the ten cords

of wood had been burned and snow was four feet deep in the woodlot. In order to conserve what wood remained, we kept a fire only in the kitchen stove. When the frost crept in during the night, the creaking of the timbers in the big house sometimes had the startling sound of a pistol shot. Nights were zero Fahrenheit, or lower, a few times touching bottom at forty below, and the days did not seem much warmer.

Upstairs in an unheated room I wore a sweater, a leather jerkin, and an overcoat while I sat at the typewriter. I kept a blanket wrapped around my feet and stopped once in a while to blow on my numb fingers. Outside the window, looking eastward, there was a great and unending expanse of crusted knee-deep snow, the monotony of its glazed whiteness broken only by stony hummocks and the outline of wind-swept, frozen gray lakes. For ten and twelve hours a day, and often through the night, I wrote story after story, revising, correcting, and rewriting with always a dogged determination, regardless of time or hardship, to keep on trying.

In February it was colder than I thought cold could get. Shivering there in the unheated room day after day, the windowpanes frosted by the vapor of my breath, the skin over my knuckles cracked by frostbite, and trying over and over again to make a story sound to the inner ear the way I wanted it to sound, I could recall very vividly the warm sunny days of midwinter in South Carolina and East Georgia.

Arthur Dolloff was provoked with me to the point of silence. He had not spoken to me since the first week in

February. The brown field rats that had moved into our cellar in November to spend the winter deserted us early in February when the cold got too much for them and all moved overnight to the warmth of the Dolloff house. Many times day and night after that could be heard the muffled sound of shotgun blasts in Arthur's cellar as he fired away in an effort to rid himself of them.

Before the end of the month we were leaving Northern New England and were on the way South. What should also have been said in the beginning was that one was more likely to be able to write in the State of Maine if he could keep warm.

II.

Restlessness, wanderlust, and an unconquerable urge to go somewhere had always kept me from being content for long at a time. When we were living in Prosperity, South Carolina, and I was six, I left home for the first time, running away to spend a day and part of a night in a livery stable before my parents could find me. When I was nine and selling afternoon newspapers in Staunton, Virginia, I got on a Chesapeake & Ohio passenger train with an armful of papers one night instead of going home; the train was stopped and I was told by the conductor never to try to ride on it again to Cincinnati in order to sell my papers. As I grew older, and I was now twenty-four years old, it became more difficult for me to stay in one place long at a time. Often I would find myself wondering what people might be doing at that moment elsewhere in America, in hundreds of villages and small towns across the country, in such cities as Denver, Grand Rapids, Spokane, Toledo, Shreveport, Des Moines, and I would want to leave right away to find out.

The fact that we had exhausted our supply of potatoes and firewood was to me not a misfortune; I now had good reason to go somewhere and the five-year-old secondhand Ford which I had bought with my savings in Atlanta had always been capable of one more trip. One of the reasons I so quickly gave up my job on the *Journal*, I suppose, was because I had to have freedom to travel whenever I could make the opportunity. And the occupation of writing, it seemed to me, was not one that required a settled existence.

I went first to Charlottesville and then to Augusta. For several weeks I lived in a one-room cabin in the piney woods near Morgana, Edgefield County, South Carolina, eating a can of pork-and-beans three times a day and writing for sixteen or eighteen hours at a time. After a while I went to Baltimore and lived on lentils and wrote short stories in a room on Charles Street. When money gave out, it was spring. I returned to Maine.

This time, early in June, endlessly fighting black flies in the woodlot, I began cutting rock maple, sawing it into heater chunks, and seasoning it in the sun and wind. I would cut wood during the day and hoe potatoes in the long purple twilight, and, when night came, I would sit down and work on a short story. At that time of the year, in that latitude, it was broad daylight at three o'clock in the morning when I went to sleep for a few hours. Time seemed to go so swiftly and there was so much to do that some nights I would stop the clock or turn the hour hand backward while I was at the typewriter.

I had written dozens of short stories during the past twelve months, in Mount Vernon, Augusta, Morgana, Baltimore, and I had the feeling that they were getting better, or at least more readable, all the time. For one thing, I was beginning to be able to form and shape imaginary incidents and events into the kind of story that produced the effect I wanted it to have on me as a reader. I tried to write with only myself in mind as the reader, just as if no one else would ever read it, believing that a writer himself must be pleased with a story before others could be, I had no faith in my ability to analyze fiction as a critic, and I would have been mistrustful of my own findings, but instead I looked for intensity of feeling in a story, weighing its emotional effect on some inner balance. If a story I had written appealed strongly to me, regardless of lack of conformity to the style of traditional fiction, I was amply satisfied with the result. The time would come, I hoped, when others too, not excluding editors, would accept it as being the only possible way that that particular story could have been written, either by me or by anyone else, to produce the sensation it gave.

Equally important to me was my belief that the content of a story was of greater importance, for enduring effectiveness in fiction, than the style in which it was written. Content was the basic material of fiction—the things in life that one told about, the thought and aspiration of men and women everywhere, the true-to-nature quality of fictitious characters who never once lived on earth but who gave the reader the illusion of being real people.

I was not writing about real people, then, but about the acts and desires of imaginary ones who, in a successful story or novel, were so convincingly depicted that they should seem more like actual persons than living people would be. Naturally, all fictional personages are to some extent created from the recollection or observation of living people by the author, for otherwise people in novels and short stories would have slight resemblance to human beings. In my way of writing, I strove to take directly from life those qualities and attributes in men and women that would, under the circumstances I was about to invent, produce in a telling way the ideal characters for the story I wanted to create. Rarely, if ever, was any such fictional character not a composite one.

It was during this period, the year 1927, that I began getting with some frequency short notes from editors instead of printed rejection slips. Even though no magazine actually accepted and published a story, at least now and then an editor would reject my work with comment.

There was always something, however, that prevented the story from being published; it was too long, too brief, too informally written, too grotesque for readers of the particular publication, too realistic in presentation for the tastes of the editorial board. It was surprising how many reasons, logical and farfetched, could be found for not accepting a story.

In addition to these terse editorial rejections, I sometimes received advice. I was not adverse to advice in principle, as long as it conformed in the main to what I was going ahead and do anyway, but it always seemed to me that the advice I received was surely intended for somebody else and had been directed to me in error.

One editor's advice was to make a careful study of the type of fiction that was published in his magazine and try to write as nearly like it as I could. Another said there was a good future in writing articles on assignment for certain trade publications on such subjects as home decoration, floor coverings, and furniture styling. One editor went to the trouble to write a fairly lengthy letter advising me to give up trying to write short stories, saying that in his opinion I would never be able to make a go of it and that the heartache of doggedly persisting would make my ultimate failure more difficult to bear.

All this was interesting correspondence and it gave me something to look forward to receiving in the mail, but it was neither rewarding nor promising. In order to keep several dozen short stories continuously making the rounds of editorial offices, a quantity of postage was necessary. There were certain semi-necessities of life, too, such as sugar and salt and shoes, which I felt I did not wish my family to do without. When money was needed, the only thing to do was to pack two suitcases with copies of books I had received for review, take a bus to Boston, and visit secondhand bookshops. I may not have originated the twenty-five-cent book business in America, but I believe I helped it get off to a good start in Boston.

12.

After getting in a winter's supply of well-seasoned beech and rock maple, I again went to Virginia, Georgia, and the Carolinas for several weeks and spent the time writing. Early in 1928, back in Mount Vernon, I decided the time had come to resign from the job of reviewing books without pay for *The Charlotte Observer* and *The Houston Post*. What prompted me more than anything else to do this was the fact that Cora Harris had gone away somewhere on a carefree vacation of several months and had left me with the chore of writing all the reviews during her absence. I let her know that she would have to find somebody else as soon as possible to take my place. Cora was a very pleasant person, and easy to get along with, but I had been filling two or three columns weekly for twenty-six months, book publishers were beginning to complain that my notices were unnecessarily short and snippy, and I begrudged the time it took from my own work.

The supply of twenty-five or thirty new books a week was to be cut off, and so I took stock of what I had. Not counting the books that had been taken to Boston from time to time and sold to secondhand dealers for a quarter each, the inventory showed that I had approximately twenty-five hundred copies of miscellaneous novels and non-fiction that had been published during the past two years. Twenty-five hundred times a quarter was one thing, but twenty-five hundred times an average retail price of two-fifty or three dollars was something else. I saw right away that I was going to open a bookshop somewhere, stock it with the books I had, and make an effort to pay myself for two years of book reviewing. It seemed reasonable that even after paying rent and other expenses I would be able to live for at least two years on the proceeds.

It probably would have required a lifetime for the three or four hundred literate inhabitants of Mount Vernon to take twenty-five hundred books off my hands at established list prices, and I went to investigate the outlook for the retail book business in nearby Augusta, Waterville, Lewiston, and Portland. Portland seemed to be the logical choice to make because of its larger population, and I began looking for somebody to manage the bookshop while I stayed at home and attended to my writing.

When the spring thaw was over, I went to Portland and rented a vacant store on Congress Street near Long-fellow Square. First I had a bookshop sign lettered on the window, and then I made trip after trip day and night between Mount Vernon and Portland, a distance of sixty-five miles, with the car loaded with books and personal belongings. By the time the store was ready for business, Marjory Morse, a young blue-eyed Smith College graduate who had been living in Switzerland the previous year, and who happened to be visiting in Portland at the time, was persuaded not to return home to Brookline, Massachusetts, but instead to come to work as manager of the bookshop. I went out to the house I had rented on Cape Elizabeth and sat down at my typewriter facing the alternating fog and sunshine of the Maine coast.

All seemed to go well at the bookshop until the stock became seriously depleted. Marge began complaining about the policy of not replenishing the stock. She said she did not blame customers for being irritated when they found that they could not purchase any book published prior to 1926 or any published since early in 1928. Business declined more rapidly as the vacant space on the shelves widened. Old customers gradually began making their book purchases elsewhere. By then, about half or more of the original stock of books had been disposed of.

I suspected that Marge Morse had come to work in the first place in order to have the opportunity to read all the new books as they were published, and now she began going out once or twice a day and renting the latest novels from a lending library nearby. When a customer came in and asked for a particular title recently issued, she was able to tell him all about the book, whether she recommended it or not, and what she thought of the author. But after that, if the customer said he wished to buy a copy, she would have to tell him that he could probably get it at one of the other bookshops in town. It was not long until Marge threatened to quit unless new books were stocked.

Call It Experience

By this time there were so few books in the store, and so little money taken in, that frequently there was not enough cash on hand at the end of the week to pay Marge her salary. The only thing to do then was to tell her to take an armful of books from the shelves and sell them, usually for a quarter each, to one of the secondhand dealers.

"How can a bookshop stay in business," Marge called up on the phone one day and asked, "if we sell three-dollar volumes for a quarter?"

Operating any kind of commercial enterprise was the last thing in the world I wanted to become involved with, but I still did not explain to her that the sole purpose of the bookshop, past, present, or future, was for me to be able to live on the proceeds from the sale of the review copies I had accumulated. I told Marge that I was writing short stories at Cape Elizabeth and that somebody else could worry about the bookshop at Longfellow Square. That settled the matter as far as I was concerned.

Marge phoned again a few days later.

"Erskine, there're two very nice men here now," she said in an excited voice. "Both of them say we really must have some new books right away if the shop is going to stay in business. They said they've traveled all over the United States, and have never seen a bookshop anywhere with so few books in it."

I asked her what business it was of any two men whether the store had books in it or not.

"They're in the book-publishing business and they said they want to see all booksellers prosper."

"What are their names?"

"One of them is Cecil Scott, and he's a traveling representative for The Macmillan Company. The handsome-looking man—I mean the tall one—is Henry Houghton, and he's a salesman for Houghton Mifflin. They have several large bags full of brand-new titles that haven't even been published yet. I'm just dying to read them. They don't even have them yet at the lending library across the street."

I asked Marge what they wanted to do about it.

"They want to sell us the new books, of course."

"Who's going to pay for them?"

"The bookshop, of course. Mr. Scott says other bookshops pay their bills, and that we can too if we run it on a businesslike basis and stop selling the stock for a quarter a volume to some secondhand dealer downtown."

"Ask Scott why he doesn't buy out the business and make a go of it himself—if he knows so much about it, and thinks it's such a gold mine."

"But, Erskine, we don't want to sell the business!" Marge protested excitedly. "I'd have to go back home to Brookline! I'd be bored to death in Brookline!"

"Do you think it could be run on a businesslike basis, and the bills paid?"

"I don't see why not."

"All right, Marge. You take over and be the boss. I'm out of it from now on. I'm going to write books, not buy them one day and then turn around and try to sell them the next."

"Then if we get some new books from Mr. Scott and

Mr. Houghton, do you want me to bring out some new novels for you to read?"

"No," I told her. "I don't want to see another book until one comes out with my name on it."

13.

It was not long before I became aware that all was not going well in the retail book business at Longfellow Square. I had gone one evening to visit Alfred Morang, a landscape painter, in his studio near the waterfront, and Alfred told me that he had seen Marge Morse carry an armful of books late that afternoon into one of the second-hand bookshops near his studio. This was not a good sign, and I suspected that more was needed at that point than the good will of Cecil Scott and Henry Houghton.

The next day I came into town from Cape Elizabeth and learned that not only had it once more become necessary to sell books to a secondhand dealer, but that the large stock of new books recently purchased had not been paid for. The unpaid bills amounted to about one thousand dollars. No one had any idea how the obligations could be met, but everybody agreed that something had to be done about it.

I walked down Congress Street trying to think what could be done. Ever since leaving Atlanta I had tried to live on what I had, no matter how little it was, and I still wanted to do that. Now I found myself owing money and being unable to pay it. After wandering through the streets of Portland for an hour, I decided to ask Ernest Gruening what he thought I should do. Ernest had been friendly toward me ever since I met him when I first came to Portland, and I felt I knew him well enough to take my troubles to him. He had been a newspaperman in Boston and New York for many years, and his first book, *Mexico and Its Heritage*, had just been published. He had founded *The Portland Evening News* and was then the editor of it. Several years later he became Governor of Alaska.

"That's an easy matter to take care of," Ernest said with an expansive gesture of his arms when I finished telling him what the difficulty was. "If you're going to get anywhere as a writer, you want to keep that kind of worry off your mind. Come on. We'll step across the street to the bank and get it attended to."

I hesitated to go to a bank seeking a loan, and I told him so, but Ernest was insistent. Reluctantly I walked across the street with him to the bank building. Ernest opened the door to the office of one of the vice-presidents and we went in and sat down. The vice-president, a tall dark-haired man of about forty with a friendly countenance, was talking on the telephone.

"Just go ahead and tell Phil what you need," Ernest whispered to me. "It's going to work out all right."

The vice-president was talking to a broker in Boston. I gathered from what was said on the phone that he was selling certain securities for the account of the bank. When he finished, he buzzed for his secretary. She came in immediately.

Call It Experience

"Miss Tibbetts," Phil instructed the young woman, "bring me those bonds I had on my desk this morning. I've just sold them."

The brown-haired young woman shook her head bewilderedly. "But I don't have them," she said. "They were on your desk the last time I saw them."

The vice-president and his secretary began searching for the bonds. They looked in desk drawers, on the floor, and in the wastebasket.

"I'd swear they were here this morning," Phil said after a while. "I had them right here in my own hands. Republic of Argentina. External Loan. A hundred thousand dollars face amount. And I've just sold them in Boston. They've got to be put in the mail tonight. You find them somewhere, Miss Tibbetts, and bring them to me as soon as you do."

When the secretary left, Ernest introduced me to the vice-president. After that there was a heavy silence in the room while they both waited for me to speak up and state the nature of my business. I glanced at Ernest and nervously shook my head. I wanted to get out of there as quickly as possible. Frowning, Ernest nodded to me emphatically.

Somehow I managed to explain that the bookshop needed money to pay its outstanding bills.

"Give me the approximate figure of your accounts receivable," Phil said as he began to open drawers again and look for the bonds.

I had to say that there were no accounts receivable, because no customer had opened a charge account.

"Bad," Phil said, shaking his head and looking directly at me. "Every commercial enterprise should have accounts receivable. The backbone of credit. Only way to do business." He shook his head again. "What security do you have, Caldwell?"

I had to admit that I had none. The only thing I owned was a secondhand car several years old, and it had little value.

"Bad," he said again, taking a deep breath. He turned around and began searching in the wastebasket a second time. "What in the world could happen to a hundred thousand dollars' worth of Argentine bonds in a safe place like a bank is supposed to be? If they'd get lost in a bank, what would happen to them somewhere else? I know they were here this morning. I counted them myself before I put in a call to our broker." He turned away from the wastebasket and looked at me again. "How much do you need to keep going, Caldwell?"

"About a thousand dollars," I said, wondering how he would be able to think about a loan for such an amount when a hundred times that much had been misplaced.

"How do you expect to pay off the note when it comes due, Caldwell?"

"I don't know how I'll pay it back," I admitted.

Ernest spoke up. "Erskine's a writer, Phil, and he's serious about it. He has a manager running the bookshop. All they need is a little cash to keep going. What he's interested in is being a fiction writer. You know—novels and short stories. Books and magazines."

Phil nodded to Ernest. Then he asked me, "When do you expect to pay it back?"

I thought about the question for several moments. "I don't know when I can," I said. "But I will pay it back when I make some money."

Phil stopped opening drawers and leaned back in his chair. "You know, Caldwell, I always wanted to be a writer myself. If I could turn out stories and get them published in magazines, I'd be a happy man. It's a wonderful thing to be a writer. I've tried putting stories down on paper, but somehow I just never seemed to make enough headway. The things I wrote just weren't good enough, I guess. That's probably why I'm a banker now." He shook his head to himself. "How do you know you'll ever make any money out of it? They tell me that writing is a pretty precarious way to make a living. Look at Ernest Gruening. Ernest writes books, but he runs a newspaper, too."

I told him I was going to keep at it until I did make a living.

"Do you have any idea when that will be?"

"In a year or two years. But maybe longer."

He smiled for the first time. "All right," he said, handing me a note to sign. "When you make a killing, Caldwell, come back and pay. I'll go along with you as long as you've got that kind of grit." He handed Ernest the note I had just signed. "The board of directors might feel better about it, Ernest, if you endorsed it." Before Ernest signed it, Phil reached forward and took it from him.

Call It Experience

"Never mind," he said. "Caldwell is going to take care of this himself."

Miss Tibbetts came in. "I just can't find those bonds anywhere," she said with a distracted expression. "They must be somewhere in this room."

As Ernest and I were leaving, Phil picked up the wastebasket and turned it upside down on the carpet. Then he and his secretary got down on their knees and began examining each scrap of paper in the litter.

14.

During the early part of 1929, a little more than six years after I first began trying to write fiction at the University of Virginia, I received the first letter of its kind I had ever found in the mail.

The letter was from Alfred Kreymborg and it said that he and the other two editors of *The New American Caravan*, Lewis Mumford and Paul Rosenfeld, were accepting for publication in October a short story I had submitted. The title was *Midsummer Passion* and it was a story with a Maine setting about a brief but violent incident having to do with a farmer who was passing a neighbor's house one summer afternoon. *Midsummer Passion* had been written the year before in Mount Vernon and it had been submitted to ten or twelve experimental magazines within the past twelve months. I did not discover until much later in the year that one of these little magazines, *transition*, edited and issued in

France, had retained a copy and published the same story; and, without my knowledge, had changed the title of the story to *July*.

The New American Caravan was an anthology that appeared once a year and it was not a magazine. The amount to be paid for the story was less than twenty-five dollars, but to me that was of little matter; what was of prime importance was the fact that somebody somewhere had at last accepted one of the short stories I had written. The accumulated disappointment of many years was suddenly and completely erased from memory.

As the result of the good news from Alfred Kreymborg, I began submitting stories to magazines in batches of six and seven at a time. Within six months, stories were accepted for publication in *transition, Blues, Hound and Horn, Nativity*, and *Pagany*. Even though technically I had achieved an aim, none of these publications qualified as a widely read commercial-type magazine and I still had far to go. All of these were so-called little magazines without general circulation, and payment, if any, was even smaller than that offered by *The New American Caravan*. The total amount I received that year for these first six published short stories, as I recollect, was less than a hundred dollars. I would gladly have let them be published for nothing at all, because such experimental magazines constituted the only workshop I had access to. My foremost aim in life, still, was to become an accomplished writer; if I could approach that, I felt confident that any rewards coming to me would take care of themselves.

Call It Experience

When I recovered to some extent from the excitement brought on by the letter from Alfred Kreymborg, I filled a suitcase with as many manuscripts as I could carry and took a bus to New York. I had twelve dollars, a round-trip bus ticket, and a copy of the first edition of *Sister Carrie*, by Theodore Dreiser, when I left Portland. I had hopefully saved the book, for which I had paid thirty-five cents in a secondhand bookshop in Atlanta and which was said to have a value several times its original published price, for just such an occasion, and I planned to sell it to help pay my expenses in New York.

With the affluence of an about-to-be-published author, I registered at the Manger Hotel (later The Taft) on Seventh Avenue at Fifty-first Street. The daily rate for my type of accommodation was two dollars, and I had enough money to stay four nights, even if I did not sell *Sister Carrie*, provided I limited the cost of meals and cigarettes to a dollar a day.

After the first full day in New York I had spent more than a dollar for food alone, and so I took the book to a dealer in first editions on East Fifty-ninth Street. The dealer inspected the copy and immediately declared that it had value, but just how much he was not ready to say. He suggested that I leave the book with him until the next day, and that in the meantime he would show it to a customer who lived on Long Island. I left it with the understanding that I was to come back the following morning to receive the current price.

My suitcase contained a little of everything in literary categories. I had several novelettes, portions of unfinished novels, poetry, jokes, essays, and dozens of short stories. I had no plan for disposing of these wares, but I hoped in some way to get them published. However, after several unsuccessful attempts to get into editorial offices, I realized that it was more difficult to secure the attention of an editor in person than it was by mail.

I was not familiar with the characteristic functions of literary representatives, or authors' agents, but it seemed to me then that it would be wise to make the acquaintance of one. Selecting an agent at random from the telephone book, I made an appointment to see him in his office. When I got there with my suitcase of manuscripts, the agent, whose name I have forgotten, took a long hard look at the contents and told me that I would have to leave everything for him to read at a later date. The later date was so indefinite that I decided that it was not something I wished to do. As I was leaving the office, the agent again asked me what my name was. When I told him, he remarked that there was at least one matter we would not have to worry about; he assured me that I had as good a name as any for literary purposes and that it would not be necessary to change it to something else.

The next morning I went to Fifty-ninth Street to keep the appointment with the dealer in first editions, optimistically hopeful of receiving ten or twelve dollars for the book. As soon as I spoke to him, he disclaimed any knowledge of me or of what I was talking about. Furthermore, the dealer said that he had never seen me before in his life. I reminded him of the conversation we had had the day before, I described the book I had left with him, and I even remembered well enough the tie he had been wearing to describe that, too. He angrily claimed that I was trying to make trouble of some sort and threatened to call the police if I did not leave immediately. I had no way of proving my story, and there was nothing I could do but go. I remained slightly hungry the remainder of the time in New York.

Alfred Kreymborg heard by some means that I had brought a suitcase full of unpublished manuscripts to town and he suggested that I let a publisher read several of the longer stories or novelettes. I gave one of the novelettes to Erich Posselt, an energetic, dapper young man, who was the editor of a publishing concern called The Heron Press.

It seemed to me, although I could have been wrong, that Erich had no office at all, but conducted his affairs in a taxicab. I met Erich by appointment several times, and on each occasion I recall meeting him at a specified time at a designated corner on Madison Avenue. He would drive up in a taxi, ask me to hop in, and we would ride slowly up and down Madison Avenue in the vicinity of Murray Hill for half an hour or longer while he talked and I listened. After two such meetings with Erich, I was psychologically prepared to accept his offer, on his terms, to publish the novelette I had given him to read. I was so excited by the prospect of having a book published that, if Erich had made the request, I probably would have signed over to him my rights to the whole suitcaseful of manuscripts.

When the contract was signed for the novelette, it was

then that Erich let it be known that he was going to publish the book under the title of *The Bastard*. It seemed to me to be an unusual title for a book of fiction, but I assumed that Erich knew the business of publishing far better than I.

In October, shortly after the publication of *The New American Caravan*, the novelette appeared in a costly limited edition of eleven hundred numbered copies with full-page illustrations by Ty Mahon. A few weeks later in Portland I received word from a county official that, although he made no claim to being a literary critic, he did know what he saw when he looked at pictures, and consequently considered it his duty to declare that the book should not be offered for sale in Portland.

15.

In the foggy gray autumn at Cape Elizabeth I received one morning a briefly worded letter from Maxwell Perkins, the editor-in-chief of Charles Scribner's Sons, in which he said that he had read one or two of my stories in small publications and that he would like me to let *Scribner's Magazine* see some of the unpublished stories I might have on hand. This was the first time anyone had invited me to submit manuscripts for consideration and, since *Scribner's Magazine* could undoubtedly be classified as a commercial magazine of general circulation, to me it meant an even longer step forward than the actual printing of my work in *The New American Caravan* and the little magazines.

The letter touched off a three-month orgy of writing, the intensity of which had never before been reached and which I never equaled afterward.

To begin with, I sent Max Perkins a short story a day for a week. Each story was promptly declined by return mail, but I was in no mood to accept discouragement. After that, I settled down to a strictly enforced routine of completing two short stories a week. It soon got to be too much for me to sit still at Cape Elizabeth and I felt the need to go somewhere else. Winter was coming to Mount Vernon and the woodshed was only partly filled that year. I went South again.

I went first to Morgana, but heavy rains had made the red clay road to the cabin in the piney woods impassable, and I went next to Augusta. In Augusta I found an inexpensive place to stay in a rooming house on Greene Street. There I wrote day and night for several weeks, going out twice a day and bringing back a can of beans and a loaf of bread for my meals.

It was January then and the room was unheated. I still had chilblains in hands and feet as the result of frostbite during my first winter in Northern New England. The aching chilblains became so painful at times that I complained to the landlady about the lack of heat. The landlady had already complained to me about the noise of my typewriter at two or three o'clock in the morning, and now she said that honest, hard-working people went out to a job in the daytime instead of staying in the house pecking on a typewriter at all hours of the night, and she intimated strongly that I should either get a job or move elsewhere. It was the only room in town I had been able to find for two-fifty a week, and I decided I would be better off if I withdrew my complaint and stayed.

It may have been colder in Mount Vernon, but I could not imagine it. By the end of January, which was midwinter in Maine, I was sure that I would be no colder in Mount Vernon than I was in an unheated room in Georgia. I got on a bus and arrived in Mount Vernon with portable typewriter and a suitcase of manuscripts, made my way to the door through three feet of snow, and started a fire in the kitchen stove. I cooked, ate, slept, and wrote in the snugly warm kitchen for the next six weeks.

During the preceding two months as fast as Max Perkins rejected a story I had sent it elsewhere. Most of these stories were accepted by *This Quarter*, *Pagany*, *Hound and Horn*, *Clay*, and other little magazines. By the end of February I thought I detected in Max's letters of rejection a decided softening of attitude toward my work. Stories were being returned less promptly, which I took to mean that he was giving them more consideration, and besides he seemed to have exhausted his stock of reasons for rejection. It may have been that he had become fatigued by my dogged persistence, but, nevertheless, his letters were increasingly less formal and more friendly and encouraging.

Erich Posselt asked me to send him another novelette, and I promptly did so. By the time it was published later

77

in the year, Alex Hillman, who had been one of the principal owners of The Heron Press, had for some reason taken over Erich's duties as editor. Alex formed a new publishing company and brought out the novelette, which was called *Poor Fool*, under the imprint of The Rariora Press and in a limited edition with illustrations by Alexander Couard. Alex had an office—located in a conventional building and not in a Madison Avenue taxicab—for the transaction of business; but, nevertheless, either because of the efficiency of his organization, or of the lack of it, a misunderstanding arose and I never received a copy of the book.

But at that time I was too engrossed with other matters to worry about the business details connected with the publication of a novelette. During that period the main objective in life as far as I was concerned was to break down the editorial resistance of *Scribner's Magazine*.

Week after week I wrote a new story and immediately mailed it to Max Perkins. Some of the stories had New England settings, others had Southern background. My mind seemed to find an inexhaustible supply of things to write about; the difficulty was in finding time enough in which to write as much as I wanted to during such a relatively short period as twenty-four hours had come to be. For a while I stopped winding the only clock in the house, but as even the sight of it was discomforting, I finally came to the practice of keeping it stored out of sight. As fast as a story was returned, I sent it elsewhere until it was accepted. Postage became a greater item of expense than food and cigarettes.

Call It Experience

The bookshop in Portland, even with the thousand-dollar working fund, was staggering toward its end. Practically all of the original stock of review copies had been sold, either going for the list price or for a quarter, and I felt that the bookshop had served its purpose and that the time had come to wind up the affairs of the business and close the doors. My family and I had lived for about two years at an actual cost to me of one thousand dollars, which sum I owed the bank and intended to repay in time. Marge Morse came to Mount Vernon a week later in low spirits. She reminded me, slightly accusingly, that she would have to go home to Brookline now. The only suggestion I could offer was that she persuade somebody else who had accumulated review copies of books to open a shop.

It was shortly before the March thaw when I received a letter from Max Perkins bringing word that my three-month campaign gave promise of ending in success. Max said that he had decided to accept one of my stories for publication in the magazine. One was to be taken, it was explained, but at that writing he had not made up his mind which one it would be.

By looking at the chart I kept, which traced the travels of stories from one magazine to the next, I could see that Max was holding five stories from which to make the selection. My immediate fear was that he might change his mind—that the already tottering economic structure of the nation might crumble—that anything could happen before he actually printed one of my stories in the magazine. I went to work at dusk that evening to supply him with enough material to enable him to make his choice without further delay.

After two nights and a day I had completed three new stories. These, together with three additional ones which I selected from the stack on my table, made a total of eleven stories for him to consider. And this time, instead of hurriedly getting the new stories into the mail, I thought it would be wiser to take them to New York in person. There was, I reasoned, the possibility of a train being wrecked, causing a serious delay in the delivery of the mail.

Part Two: The Middle Years

I.

During the overnight bus trip from Portland to New York, I was kept wide awake with forebodings of misfortune. By the time the bus had passed through Hartford, not long after midnight, confident aggressiveness had become a dubious asset, and I was questioning the wisdom of what I was doing. I had never seen Maxwell Perkins, my only contact with him having been through correspondence, and by daybreak I was beginning to visualize him as a fearsome person who would angrily resent the intrusion and become prejudiced against my work.

Clutching the envelope of manuscripts, I spent the time walking up and down Fifth Avenue in front of the Scribner Building from about eight until shortly after ten o'clock in the morning. For two hours I tried to think of a reasonable excuse to offer for presenting myself without invitation, but nothing would come to mind that sounded persuasive and effective. When ten o'clock passed, I crossed the street, feeling that what little remaining courage I had was rapidly vanishing, and took the elevator to the editorial offices.

A pleasant young woman immediately asked me what

I wanted. Uneasy in the surroundings and by then thoroughly unnerved, I told her merely that I wished to leave an envelope of manuscripts for Maxwell Perkins. She asked if I would like to see him, and I hastily said I did not. As I was turning to go, she asked if I would like to leave a message with the envelope. I spelled out my name and said that I was going to be at the Manger Hotel for the next two days. Then I hurriedly took the elevator down.

When I got to the hotel, I went to my room and sat down to wait. Reason told me that it was foolish to be waiting, but nevertheless I could not admit to myself that the trip had been in vain, and I hoped that Max Perkins would phone me there instead of writing a note to me at Mount Vernon. I left the room only long enough to hurry down to the street and eat a sandwich and buy several newspapers, and at nightfall I went to bed and lay tensely awake until past midnight trying to find the necessary courage to phone Max Perkins if he should fail to call me before I left town.

At six-thirty I was up the next morning. I had eaten breakfast, bought more newspapers, and was back in my room waiting again by eight o'clock. It was midmorning when the phone rang. The sound was startling at first, but it was so pleasing to hear that I let the phone ring twice before answering it; I was certain there was only one person in all of New York who would be calling me.

As I remember it, the conversation was like this:

Perkins: Caldwell? Erskine Caldwell, from Mount Vernon, Maine?

Call It Experience

Caldwell: Yes.

Perkins: Well, how are you, Caldwell? It's Perkins. Max Perkins. Scribner's.

Caldwell: I'm all right, I guess.

Perkins: I got your new manuscripts yesterday, the ones you left at the office. I wish you had asked for me when you were here.

Caldwell: Well—you did?

Perkins: By the way, I've read all your stories on hand now, including the new ones you brought yesterday, and I don't think I need to see any more for a while.

Caldwell: (Silence).

Perkins: I think I wrote you some time ago that we want to publish one of your stories in *Scribner's Magazine.*

Caldwell: I received the letter. You haven't changed your mind, have you? I mean, about taking a story.

Perkins: Changed my mind? No. Not at all. The fact is, we're all in agreement here at the office about your things. I guess so much so that we've decided now to take two stories, instead of one, and run them both in the magazine at the same time. We'd like to schedule them for the June issue. One of them is called *The Mating of Marjorie* and the other one is *A Very Late Spring.* They're both good Northern New England stories. There's something about them that appeals strongly to me.

There's a good feeling about them. It's something I like to find in fiction. So many writers master form and technique, but get so little feeling into their work. I think that's important.

Caldwell: I'm sure glad you like them—both of them.

Perkins: You're going to keep on, aren't you? Writing, I mean. You'll keep it up, won't you? We want to see some more of your work, later.

Caldwell: I'm going to keep on writing—I'm not going to stop.

Perkins: That's good to hear.

Caldwell: (Silence).

Perkins: Now about these two stories. As I said, we want to buy them both. How much do you want for the two together? We always have to talk about money sooner or later. There's no way of getting around that, is there?

Caldwell: Well, I don't know exactly. I mean, about the money. I hadn't thought much about it.

Perkins: Would two-fifty be all right? For both of them.

Caldwell: Two-fifty? I don't know. I thought maybe I'd receive a little more than that.

Perkins: You did? Well, what would you say to three-fifty then? That's about as much as we can pay, for both of them. In these times magazine circulation is not climbing the way it was, and we have to watch our costs. I don't think times will get any better soon, and maybe worse yet. Economic life isn't very healthy now. That's why we have to figure our costs closely at a time like this.

Caldwell: I guess that'll be all right. I'd thought I'd get a little more than three dollars and a half, though, for both of them.

Perkins: Three dollars and fifty cents? Oh, no! I must have given you the wrong impression, Caldwell. Not three dollars and a half. No. I meant three hundred and fifty dollars.

Caldwell: You did! Well, that's sure different. It sure is. Three hundred and fifty dollars is just fine. I didn't expect that much.

Perkins: All right then. I'll have a check drawn and it'll be in the mail in a few days. Where should it be sent? Where'll you be staying?

Caldwell: I'm going back to Mount Vernon. I'll probably take the night boat on the Fall River Line.

Perkins: Do you always take the boat? Is that the way you travel?

Caldwell: This is the first time. The bus is a lot cheaper. But maybe I can afford it now.

Perkins: Well, good-by, Caldwell. Send us some more stories, after a breathing spell, when you have them. It's good to know you'll keep on writing. And come in to see me the next time you're in town. Good-by.

Call It Experience

Caldwell: I'll certainly send some more stories. Good-by.

Perkins: You do that. Good-by, again.

2.

In due time the stories appeared in the June issue of *Scribner's Magazine*. It was a satisfying feeling to know that I had reached the goal I had set out for in the beginning, but, now that it had been attained, I could think of other goals farther in the distance that seemed to be much more important. I thought one of these to strive for should be the writing and publication of one hundred short stories.

It was the beginning of summer then and once more I took up my habit of cutting wood during the day, cultivating potatoes by twilight, and writing at night. Instead of working furiously now to produce a quantity of short stories, I limited myself to the writing of one story a week; and because I could devote more time to an individual story, I found that the things I did were more satisfactory in the end.

Each new story was sent promptly to Max Perkins, but none was taken. After a story was returned, I mailed it to one of the little magazines, and in almost each instance it was published by one of them. There were a dozen or more such publications flourishing then, and new ones appeared at frequent intervals. At the stage of writing that I was in, I made no attempt to get my work into the mass-circulation periodicals, as I believed that there was more to be gained in the end by first being thoroughly schooled by the literary magazines. I now made it a practice, when a story was declined by any six magazines, to destroy it and abandon the idea on which it had been based. I never regretted that I followed this plan.

After the Fourth of July, 1930, I left the big summer house and moved down the hill to a small cottage on Parker Lake where I would be able to go swimming between chores of writing and physical labor. I had been so engrossed in writing and submitting manuscripts during the past several years that I had not stopped to go back and re-read what I had written during that time. Now I gathered all the manuscripts, which included novels and novelettes as well as other material, and took them to the cottage to read. There were nearly three suitcases full of manuscripts of unpublished work, but after a night of sampling of it, I was so dissatisfied with my past work that the next morning I carried everything down to the shore of the lake and burned it. The poetry, jokes, and essays were the first to go into the fire.

And while I was about it, and for good measure, I added to the bonfire the complete collection of rejection slips I had accumulated during the past seven years.

A few weeks after burning the manuscripts I received a letter from Max Perkins in which he said that he had been thinking about the stories I had submitted recently and that he now thought it would be a good idea to bring out a collection of them in book form after the first of the year. He suggested that I get together a sufficient number of stories, previously published in magazines and unpublished ones as well, to make a book of two hundred and fifty or three hundred pages.

Fifteen stories had either been published or accepted for publication in various magazines. One of these was *Story*, the most recently founded and most promising of the little magazines. It was ably edited by Whit Burnett and Martha Foley. To these fifteen I added ten new stories. It so happened that about half of the stories had New England settings and the other half had Southern background. After thinking about it for several days I decided I wanted to call the book *American Earth*.

The typing and revising of the manuscript, which was approximately two hundred and seventy-five pages in length, required three weeks or more, and it was late summer when I went to Boston and took the Eastern Steamship Line night boat to New York.

This time I did not hesitate to call on Max Perkins. He greeted me cordially in his sparsely furnished office when I went in and handed him the manuscript of *American Earth*. Wearing a hat with a turned-up brim, which appeared to be at least half a size too small for him, he sat down at his desk and slowly turned the pages of the manuscript for a quarter of an hour. No word was spoken while he sat there. At the end of that time he got up smiling a little and moved stiffly around his office in new bright-tan shoes, occasionally looking out his window at the traffic below, while he told of several incidents he recalled about life in Vermont when he was a youth.

After nearly an hour of reminiscing, sometimes seriously and often humorously, he mentioned for the first time the manuscript I had brought. All he said then was that Scribner's would want to publish it, probably in the spring of the following year, 1931, and that he would want to choose perhaps two of the unpublished stories to run in the magazine prior to publication in book form.

As I was getting ready to leave, he mentioned the matter of a contract for the book and asked if I had any suggestions to make concerning it. I told him I had none, except that I needed a little money to live on and that I would appreciate an advance royalty payment. First he cautioned me not to expect any large sale of a book of short stories, saying that the book-buying public preferred novels and that the royalty would do well to amount to two hundred or two hundred and fifty dollars, and then he promised to have a small advance payment made, saying that the check would be sent with the contract when it was ready for my signature about the first of October. I was pleased with the prospect of receiving as much as two hundred and fifty dollars, and after leaving the office I went down to the Providence Line pier and bought a ticket on the night boat.

The contract for *American Earth* and the check for the advance royalty payment were sent to me promptly, and as soon as I received the money I began making plans to take a trip somewhere. I had had little opportunity to travel recently, except between Maine and New York by bus or boat, and now I wanted to go on a trip to the Pacific Coast. I had never been west of the Mississippi River and I had been looking forward to seeing other regions of America for a long time. After making a barrel of cider and storing it in the cellar, I was ready to leave. Early in October, taking my Corona portable typewriter, a Target cigarette-making machine, and a suitcase, I left Maine on a bus for California.

3.

By traveling continuously, and avoiding the expense of stopping at hotels along the way, the trip from Portland to Los Angeles could have been made in five days and six nights. The expense was an important matter, because I had left Mount Vernon with only enough money, after spending about a hundred dollars for a round-trip bus ticket, to enable me to live on twelve or thirteen dollars a week while writing during the next three months. In addition to the typewriter, the other assets I had, which were carried in the suitcase, were an extra typewriter ribbon, two reams of yellow second sheets, and a month's supply of tobacco and cigarette papers for the cigarette-making machine.

I stopped in Boston, New York, Pittsburgh, and St. Louis only long enough to change to a connecting transcontinental bus. The excitement of traveling across the country for the first time kept me awake all the way to

New York, I dozed fitfully in the lurching bus for a few hours the second night, and when I got to St. Louis, after a completely sleepless third night, I was beginning to wonder how sane it was to try to save money by living aboard a bus for nearly a week. However, in St. Louis the connecting bus to Kansas City was waiting, and I got on it.

The two hundred and fifty miles between the two cities seemed like the total distance of all the traveling I had done during my life. After the all-day ride it was dusk when I staggered off the bus in Kansas City and lugged the typewriter and suitcase to the Pickwick Hotel.

In my dazed, blear-eyed, sleepless state after three days and three nights of travel it was not clear then, nor was it any too clear afterward, what were the separate details that went to make up the complete list of events that took place during the next six hours. Many times since I have tried to recall the happenings of the evening step by step, but always now, as it must have come to pass then, there are indescribable gaps in the whole piece of my consciousness. The reason for these lapses must surely have been because I was unable to keep my eyes open much of the time that evening.

I did register at the Pickwick Hotel, though, and I was taken to my room by a bellboy. Both of us, one after the other, stumbled over some baggage before the light switch could be located; there were five or six heavy cases of various dimensions on the floor near the door. The bellboy phoned down to the desk clerk to find out if a mistake had been made when I was assigned to the room, and he was told that the room had been vacated, but permission had been given to leave the baggage there temporarily. It was further explained that the contents of the cases were said by the owner to be valuable, and that the baggage would probably be sent for within the next ten or fifteen minutes.

It was a pleasantly decorated room with an inviting bed and softly shaded lighting. As soon as the bellboy left, I turned on the shower and got ready to shave for the first time in three days. I was in the shower when somebody knocked on the door.

Opening the door a little, I saw a slender, brunet, trimly dressed young woman, who appeared to be in her middle twenties, standing in the hall. She could not be described as plain-looking or uninteresting.

"Have you moved in here?" the girl said with an annoyed frown.

I nodded.

There was a pause of several moments. After that she said, "I had it till six o'clock and then I checked out so they wouldn't charge me for another night. All those cases belong to me, and I only wanted to leave them here till train time. But the train I'm taking to Tulsa is late. They say it'll be another two hours before it leaves. Would you mind if my cases stay here a little while longer?"

I told her it would be all right as far as I was concerned.

."Thank you a lot," she said, smiling friendlily. "That's awfully good of you. It's a big help. I don't like to check them downstairs. I lost one of my biggest cases that way not long ago. Is it all right for me to come in and get something out of one of them? You don't mind, do you?"

I said it would be all right, and went back into the shower and closed the bathroom door. After ten minutes I opened the door and looked into the room. The young woman had taken off her coat and was sitting in one of the chairs reading a magazine.

"You probably want to come in now, don't you?" she said, smiling again. "I'll leave so I won't bother you any more."

She went out into the hall and closed the door. I did not take time to lock the room or turn out the lights but fell, exhausted and sleepy, across the bed. It seemed as though only a few moments had passed when I became conscious of somebody shaking me determinedly. I opened my eyes enough to see the dark-haired young woman bending over me.

"What's the matter?" I asked sleepily.

"That Tulsa train is going to be another hour late," she said with a frown. "They said it won't leave till tenthirty. I hate to sit in the lobby all that time."

"What are you going to do about it?"

"Would it be all right for me to stay here?" She looked at me appealingly. "I'll just sit here and read."

I lay there gazing at her momentarily, and then I was asleep again. The next I knew, I was being shaken awake. The girl was sitting on the side of the bed this time.

"What's the matter with you?" I heard her ask.

"Sleepy," I muttered.

"It's only nine-thirty. I just phoned the station, and

that Tulsa train won't leave till eleven-thirty. It makes me so mad!"

"Why?" I said.

"Wouldn't it make you mad? Suppose you had a lot of calls to make in Tulsa tomorrow morning, and then had to get to Oklahoma City and make a lot more before night."

"What kind of calls?" I asked her.

She nodded in the direction of the cases stacked near the door. "I sell beauty-shop supplies," she said. "That's my line. I've got seven good accounts in Tulsa, and just as many in Oklahoma City. Those people in that business buy hand-to-mouth, and if I don't make my calls regularly, somebody else comes along and takes the business away from me."

I nodded and closed my eyes wearily. I fell asleep again, but I was soon awakened.

"What's your line?" the girl asked. "You travel, don't you?"

I nodded. "I travel."

"What do you sell?"

"Paper—with words on it."

"How's that?" she asked interestedly. "What do you mean?"

I was asleep again before I could make a reply. I woke up finding her shaking me. Her persistence in trying to make me stay awake was getting to be torment. I tried to push her away.

Giggling a little, she said, "We ought to get to know each other better. What's your name?"

"Skinny," I said, my eyelids falling shut.

She laughed. "That must be a nickname."

I nodded my head the best I could.

"My name is Edna." She shook me insistently until I opened my eyes. "I'm going to phone down and have some beer sent up. I wouldn't mind having a party, would you? That train's marked up to leave at twelve-thirty now. There's plenty of time."

I could hear faintly the sound of Edna talking to somebody on the phone after that, but I remembered nothing more until once again I was shaken insistently. When I opened my eyes, she leaned over and whispered something, but her voice sounded far away and I did not bother to listen to what she was saying. Partly awake and partly asleep, I thought I could taste beer, but I was not certain. Then sometime later, as though a heavy weight had been put upon me, I found myself struggling frantically for breath; but not long after that I felt the pleasant sensation of falling endlessly through space and all consciousness vanished.

When I woke up the next time, it was dawn. The sample cases and Edna were no longer in the room. I turned over and went back to sleep.

4.

Twenty-four hours after arriving in Kansas City, at least half of the time having been devoted exclusively to sleep, I felt fully capable of completing the last half of the trip to the West Coast without stopping again. Three nights and three days later, after having changed busses in Denver and again in Salt Lake City, and after having been stalled for seven hours in an unheated bus in a snowdrift during a Wyoming blizzard, I arrived in Los Angeles. It was early afternoon then, and in the balmy California autumn I felt as if I would have gone to sleep on the sidewalk if I had not forced myself to keep in motion. I was more blear-eyed and drowsy from lack of sleep than I had been when I stopped in Kansas City.

After walking several blocks with suitcase and typewriter, I still had not seen a hotel, and I asked somebody where I could find one that had inexpensive rooms. The man I spoke to promptly suggested that I take a streetcar to Hollywood, saying that more hotels could be found there than on Spring Street in Los Angeles.

The streetcar had passed Vine Street and the center of Hollywood when I saw a sign on a building about a block south of Hollywood Boulevard that advertised the Mark Twain Hotel. I immediately thought of a memorable short story by Mark Twain that I had read at the University of Virginia, which made a hotel bearing his name seem like a place where a writer would feel at home, and so I got off at the next stop and walked back to the hotel.

The Mark Twain was a small, white stucco hotel on Wilcox Avenue. I judged by its appearance that its rates might be in keeping with my ability to pay, and as soon as I walked into the lobby the desk clerk cheerfully handed me a pen and asked me to register. It was then that I inquired about the cost of a room by the week or month. The rates he proposed were higher than I felt I could afford, and I hesitated to sign the register.

"Payable in advance, of course," the clerk continued.

"But I've got baggage," I said.

I watched him lean over the desk and look disapprovingly at my scarred and worn suitcase and typewriter case.

"That's a typewriter you've got there," he stated in an accusing manner.

I nodded, and at the same time wondered why a clerk in a hotel named for Mark Twain would have such an unfriendly attitude toward a typewriter.

"And you're a writer, aren't you?"

I nodded again.

"I'm sorry," he said, turning partly away. "We don't have anything available just now—by the month."

"I'll take a room by the week then," I told him.

"Nothing right now," he said shortly, shaking his head.

"Then just give me a room for the night," I said desperately. "I've got to have a place to sleep—I can't stay awake any longer."

"You'd better try somewhere else," he told me. "You'll find several hotels along the street."

"Why can't I get a room here?"

"Because we've had nothing but trouble with writers, that's why. They've been coming here and running up bills and then skipping out without paying. All we ever find after they've gone is an empty suitcase. They always manage to get away with their typewriters somehow."

I picked up the typewriter and suitcase and walked

down the street. At the corner near Sunset Boulevard I
went into the lobby of the Warwick Hotel. It may not
have been smaller than the Mark Twain, but it looked
more like a residential hotel than one for transients. A
pleasant woman of about thirty-five with ringlets of
blond curls came up and asked if I wanted a room.

As soon as I told her that I was looking for an inexpensive room on a weekly or monthly rate basis, she said
that she had a room I could take for seven dollars a week.
I hurriedly signed the register before the subject of typewriters could be brought up and handed her seven dollars.

When I saw her looking interestedly at the address I
had written on the register, I picked up my baggage and
carried it to the upper floor. After a delay of several minutes, the blond-haired woman came up the stairs in a rustle
of skirts and, while saturating the air with a pungent per-
fume, unlocked the door of my room.

"Where did you say you're from?" she asked, going
to the bed and carefully smoothing the magenta spread.

"The State of Maine," I told her.

"Are you sure?" she asked, looking up and shaking
her head a little.

I told her I was certain.

She said nothing more after that, and after she had
gone, I locked the door and went to the window. It was
twilight then and the rose-tinted glow of lights over
Hollywood made me want to go out to see the town,
but I knew I was going to fall asleep any minute. I could
barely keep my eyes open then. After rolling a cigarette

with the cigarette-making machine, I lit it and dropped wearily to the side of the large bed.

I remembered nothing after that until I was partly awakened several hours later by a noisy commotion in the hall just outside my door. In addition to banging loudly on the door, several persons were shouting at the top of their voices. For a while I thought surely I was dreaming, because I was certain that no hotel, not even a Hollywood hotel, would tolerate guests who made such a disturbance in the middle of the night. The clamor and shouting increased, and as I finally opened my eyes, wondering if this could actually be a Hollywood party after all, a fireman splintered the wooden door with an ax.

A moment later the room was crowed with a dozen or more excited men and women, most of whom were in pajamas or bathrobes. I was aware of the odor of burning cotton by then, but I had no idea that anything in my room was burning until the two firemen jerked me to my feet and shook me hard. While that was happening, several buckets of water were splashed on the smoldering bed. Then I saw that about half of the mattress of the wide double bed had burned completely, leaving only the bedsprings to be seen on one side of it.

"The poor boy!" I heard the pleasant-voiced woman say somewhere in the room. "I could tell by looking at him that he was dog-tired and sleepy when he came here this afternoon. Is he burned anywhere?"

The firemen looked at my face, arms, and clothing. "I don't see how he kept from getting burned," one of them said. "He doesn't know how lucky he is. Another half hour—and he would've been burned for sure."

"I'm going to move him to another room and let him get some sleep," the woman said. "The poor boy!"

"Don't you want to do something about him—for setting the bed on fire?" one of the firemen asked her. "That could've burned down the whole hotel—if somebody hadn't smelled the smoke in time."

"No," she told him, picking up my suitcase and typewriter.

"Looks like you'd want to call the police, or make him pay for the damage," the other fireman said.

"No," she said firmly, pushing me toward the hall. "He said he came here from Maine, but he can't fool me. He talks just like anybody in Georgia, and I'm from Georgia, too. After living out here among strange people as long as I have, the last thing I'd do would be to make trouble for somebody from back home."

5.

The urge to write was stronger than any desire to see the renowned sights of Hollywood, and I was rarely out of my room at the Warwick for more than an hour at a time. When I did leave it, I usually went to a drugstore on the corner for a fifteen-cent breakfast or for a twenty-cent lunch, and in the late afternoon or early evening I went two blocks up the street to a restaurant on Hollywood Boulevard where a platter of T-bone steak and hash-browned potatoes cost only twenty cents. The twenty-cent steak was far from being tender, but it made a filling meal. I was living well within my budget of twelve dollars a week, and besides had enough money left over to buy tobacco for my cigarette-making machine and to provide postage for the stories I was submitting to experimental magazines almost daily.

After six weeks at the Warwick Hotel, it became clear in my mind that I was dissatisfied with the progress I was making. It was during this time in October and November that I had gradually come to realize that I would not be completely satisfied with any of my work until I had written a full-length novel and, moreover, that it was inevitable that the novel was to be concerned with the tenant farmers and sharecropping families I had known in East Georgia.

Even though I had been away from Wrens and Jefferson County for a long time, I felt that I would never be able to write successfully about other people in other places until first I had written the story of the landless and poverty-stricken families living on East Georgia sand hills and tobacco roads. The novels I had read as a reviewer seemed even more remote from life now than they had at the time I read them; in retrospect they seemed more concerned with contrived situations and artificial events than with reality.

I wanted to tell the story of the people I knew in the manner in which they actually lived their lives from day to day and year to year, and to tell it without regard for fashions in writing and traditional plots. It seemed to me that the most authentic and enduring materials of fiction were the people themselves, not crafty plots and counterplots designed to manipulate the speech and actions of human beings. My mind was made up. I packed my suitcase and, traveling through Arizona, New Mexico, and Texas, went back to Georgia.

It was December when I arrived at my parents' home in Wrens. The weather had turned damp and cold and the cotton fields were brown and the dogwood hedges dormant.

Within a few miles from town, families on tenant farms were huddled around fireplaces in drafty hovels. Most of them were despondent. Some were hungry as usual; others were ill and without medical attention. Food and clothing were scarce, and in some instances nonexistent; jobs were rarely to be found. It was not a pleasant sight, more dispiriting to look upon now than it had been several years before. I could not keep from recalling Max Perkins's observation that the economic life of the nation was not healthy and would perhaps not improve for a long time; economic life on tenant and sharecropping farms in East Georgia had not been healthy for a long, long time.

Day after day I went into the country, becoming more depressed by what I saw as I traveled farther and farther from settlements and highways. I could not become accustomed to the sight of children's stomachs bloated from hunger and seeing the ill and aged too weak to walk to the fields to search for something to eat. In the evenings I wrote about what I had seen during the day, but nothing I put down on paper succeeded in conveying the full meaning of poverty and hopelessness and degradation as I had observed it. The more I traveled through Burke, Jefferson, and Richmond Counties, the less satisfied I became with what I wrote. In my mind, there was a foreordained story to be told, and it had to be related as the people themselves knew it. Finally, knowing it was something I was impelled to do before I could ever write about anything else, I left Wrens and went to New York. The perspective I gained by going there was what I had been seeking.

I rented a hall bedroom on the fourth floor of a brownstone house between Fifth and Sixth Avenues on the present site of Rockefeller Center. The room was small, there being only enough space for a narrow bed, a lamp table, and a chair, but it had a view of the brownstone fronts across the street.

The buildings in the locality were to be torn down to make way for the skyscrapers of Radio City, and rents in the meantime were low. The rent for my room was three dollars and a half weekly. I was able to live on fifty cents a day for food, chiefly by buying a loaf of rye bread and a pound of daisy cheese and eating it in my room. Once a day, usually in the late afternoon, I went to a nearby restaurant on Sixth Avenue, later renamed The Avenue of the Americas, and paid ten cents for a bowl of lentil soup and a nickel for a cup of coffee. By spending only seven dollars a week for room and food, five dollars a week less than I had spent in California, I had sufficient money to live there during the winter months from January to April.

To begin with I had spent fifty cents for a new type-writer ribbon, a quarter for a water-stained ream of yellow second sheets, and a nickel for two pencils. Then I destroyed everything I had written while I was in Georgia. When I was ready to start writing, I typed the title I had decided upon while riding on the bus to New York. There was only one possible title for the novel; it was to be called *Tobacco Road*. The term tobacco road had originally been applied to thoroughfares that had been made by rolling heavy hogsheads of tobacco along high ridges from East Georgia farms to the Savannah River, but when such roads were no longer used for that purpose, they reverted to landowners who did not keep them in repair.

There was never any doubt in my mind about the outcome of the novel from that time until I finished the first draft of it three months later. My daily habit, seven days a week, was to get up before noon, eat bread and cheese, and start writing. The story I wanted to tell was so vivid in my mind that I did not take the time to go back and read what I had written the day before. I usually stopped writing for an hour in the late afternoon to eat soup and take a walk along one of the streets in the Fifties, and then came back and wrote and rewrote until three or four o'clock in the morning. As soon as a chapter was finished, I revised it until I was satisfied with the way it read, and then began the next chapter. When the stack of second sheets began to dwindle, I used the reverse side of them in order to conserve paper.

I felt no loneliness during that period early in 1931, probably because I was so deeply absorbed in what I was doing, and I had occasion to meet only a few persons connected with writing and publishing, even refraining from phoning or going to see Max Perkins. I spent one evening talking to Raymond Everitt and Charles A. Pearce, both of whom were editors at the publishing house of Harcourt, Brace and Company, and late in March I attended a cocktail party at the offices of The Macaulay Company, publishers of *The American Caravan.*

There were two chief attractions, as far as I was concerned, at this party. One of these was a well-provisioned buffet table that provided the only full meal I had had in nearly three months, and the other attraction was Mae West. Fully fed and having gazed to my heart's content upon Mae West, my mind was then able to retain the experience of meeting some of the other guests, among them being Laurence Stallings, Robert Cantwell, Mike Gold, Edwin Seaver, Georges Schreiber, Dawn Powell, Lewis Mumford, John Chamberlain, Georgia O'Keeffe, and Edmund Wilson.

It was at this same gathering that I met Maxim Lieber, who had been an editor at the publishing house of Brentano's, and who was founding an authors' literary agency. Max Lieber was the first agent to invite me to become a client, and the offer was such a surprise to me that I was unable to believe it was a genuine one. I told Max that I thought I should consider it for a while. I was afraid that he was making merely a friendly social gesture and that the offer would soon be forgotten, but a few months later Max wrote and asked me what decision I had come to. I quickly wrote in reply that I wanted to become associated with him, if he were still so minded, and from that time forward Max Lieber handled all my domestic and foreign contracts and negotiations for books and short stories.

The first draft of *Tobacco Road*, which was about two hundred pages in length, was finished the first week in April, 1931, and I had just enough money left to buy a bus ticket to Mount Vernon. *American Earth* was published later in the same month, I received three hundred and fifty dollars from *Scribner's Magazine* for two stories published that spring, and Max Perkins, after publication of the book of short stories, wrote to ask how I felt about writing a novel. I did not tell him that I had already finished the first draft of one, but I did say that I hoped to be able to send him the completed manuscript of a novel before the end of summer.

6.

The newspaper and magazine reviews of *American Earth* were of a so-called mixed nature. That is to say, some of the reviews were favorable and sympathetic; the larger portion were not. I had not expected an avalanche of unstinted praise for this volume of short stories, because I was well aware of some of its short-comings, but I was unprepared for the large proportion of unfavorable criticism.

My own experience as a reviewer had kept me from anticipating nothing but praise, but it was a revelation to find that the majority of reviewers, when not unconsciously demonstrating an ignorance of their calling, were often contemptuous or sadistic in their appraisal of a book of fiction. The notices of my book were not unique in this respect. I found by reading reviews of other authors' books that supercilious treatment was a common pattern. There seemed to be reasonable evidence, after all, that there might be some truth in the belief that a good many reviewers and critics were impotent lovers or unsuccessful authors. Perhaps a would-be reviewer or critic should be required to demonstrate his ability either to make love or else to write a publishable book of fiction.

With the exception of Gorham Munson, Horace Gregory, William Soskin, James Gray, and Harry Emerson Wildes, as well as several others who wrote perceptive notices, the reviewers for the most part looked upon *American Earth* with disdain. Beyond that point the majority of them appeared to be blind to their critical obligation to tell their readers something concerning the contents of the book and in what manner and to what degree the author had failed or succeeded in his attempt to write interesting fiction. The book, not necessarily because of the reviews, had a sale of less than a thousand copies.

Call It Experience

After reading a sizable batch of these reviews from many parts of the nation, I no longer had respect for the profession of reviewing, and day by day my regard for it diminished. As a result of this, I became convinced that the average book-review column, page, or supplement was a pitiful stepchild of American journalism, grievously mistreated year after year by impassive editors and psychopathic reviewers alike.

Following the experience of reading the reviews of *American Earth*, I went to work on the second draft of *Tobacco Road* with a better understanding of what I wished to accomplish. Until this time I had been apprehensive of the reception of my work by the critics, foolishly believing that a writer's success depended to a large degree upon his ability to win the favor of those who wrote reviews of his books. Now I had no such handicap. And at the same time I had learned a valuable lesson. It was now my conviction that a writer's obligation was to himself and to his readers, and that all his effort should be directed toward those two. Thereafter, in my credo, reviewers could look elsewhere for bootlicking; readers were to be the ones to pass final judgment on my books.

There was wood to be cut that spring and summer, and potatoes to be grown. I found that the most profitable division of time during this period was to devote eight hours a day to sleep, eight hours to writing, and eight hours to physical labor. By the end of July the second and final draft of *Tobacco Road* had been finished, the woodshed was filled with sawn beech and maple, and the garden was free of potato bugs.

I had written no short stories since leaving California in November, having devoted the past eight months to work on the novel, but, even so, stories previously written were being accepted and published in greater number than they had been the year before. These were appearing in *Pagany, Clay, Story, This Quarter, Nativity,* and *Scribner's Magazine.* One of these stories, *Dorothy,* which had been published that spring in *Scribner's,* was selected to be reprinted in *The Best Short Stories of 1931,* edited by Edward J. O'Brien. After sending off the manuscript of the novel, I again returned to writing short stories.

Less than two weeks after the manuscript had been sent away, I received a briefly worded note from Max Perkins in which he said that *Tobacco Road* was being accepted and would be published in book form by Charles Scribner's Sons early the following year. He wrote, further, that the manuscript needed no editing before sending it to the printer, and that consequently it was not necessary to suggest any changes or revisions.

I felt that I could safely count on receiving an advance royalty payment when I asked for it, and so I got ready to leave Mount Vernon. I had been there this time for almost five months, and that was a long time for me to stay in one place. Carrying my suitcase and typewriter, and not forgetting the cigarette-making machine, I left for New York after Labor Day.

Call It Experience

7.

When I arrived in New York in September of 1931, I stayed for several days at the Manger Hotel while looking for an inexpensive room in a quiet location. The rooms in the area where I had lived for three months during the past winter were still cheap, but the dwellings were rapidly coming down and the incessant din of drilling day and night made living there, even temporarily, far from desirable. When I told Max Lieber that I could no longer afford the expense of staying at the Manger, which was at a rate of about fourteen dollars weekly, he suggested that we go to see Nathanael West.

Nathanael West, who was better known as Pep West, had published a novel which many critics had been prone to disparage by calling it esoteric; thus labeled, the book had not been widely read. The author had not been embittered by the notices of the reviewers, but he was puzzled by their unsympathetic attitude and by the lack of understanding of his purpose.

Besides being a writer, Pep was the manager of an exclusive residential hotel, the Sutton, in the East Fifties. He knew the financial hardships under which most young authors worked and, being a close relative of the owner of the hotel, he was in a position to make attractive rates for writers during that period of economic weakness in the early Thirties. It was said to be good business for a hotel at that time to be filled as completely as possible by paying, partially paying, or even by some non-paying guests. I do not know how many authors and would-be authors Pep helped in this manner during the depression of the era, but for several years the Sutton was one of the few hotels of its type that had more lighted windows at night than dark windows.

Although Pep West was agreeable to my moving into the Sutton, he refused to set a price for a room or even to hint at one, saying that I could pay whatever I could afford. Knowing something of the established rates at the Sutton, I was ashamed to tell him that four dollars a week, possibly five dollars, was my limit. However, urged by Max Lieber not to lose such an opportunity, I moved into a luxuriously decorated room in the hotel that same day.

After being in the Sutton a week, I went to the cashier and offered ten dollars in payment for a week's rent. Nothing was said to embarrass me, but none the less I felt uncomfortable. I knew that, while I was paying twice as much as I could afford, it was several times less than the established rate called for.

During this period Pep was working on a novel that later was published under the title of *Miss Lonelyhearts,* but he was dissatisfied with his progress and twice destroyed drafts of it. He said each time I talked to him that he wanted to leave New York and finish the novel somewhere in the country. I myself was dissatisfied with the progress I was making and had been unable to finish more than a few pages of the novel I planned to write in New York that winter. For one thing, I felt too ill at ease under the circumstances and realized that I should move from the Sutton and make a new start on the novel elsewhere. Eating bread and cheese in one of the hotel's richly carpeted rooms was more than I could continue doing; no matter how much water I drank, the food was increasingly difficult to swallow.

After staying at the Sutton for three weeks, I told Pep that I would have to move to less expensive living quarters. He urged me to stay, saying that as far as he was concerned I could pay a dollar a week or nothing a week, but nevertheless I packed my suitcase and left.

This time I went across town to the West Eighties and rented a hall bedroom on the third floor of a brownstone front half a block from Central Park. The rent there was four dollars and a half weekly.

With the experience of writing *Tobacco Road* still dominating my mind and thought, I undertook to readjust myself by writing the next novel about life in some part of the country other than the South. The first novel had not yet been published, and would not appear until February of 1932, but I had been so absorbed in the story and so anxious to write it well that I was afraid any book I wrote about the South at this time would be less forceful and, consequently, less effective. The story I then set out to write was about a family in the State of Maine.

Having spent twice as much money as I had intended during the first month in New York, I tried to live even more frugally than I had earlier in the year. I still ate rye bread and rat-trap cheese in my room, but less of it, and when I went out in the late afternoon, I paid a dime for a bowl of navy bean soup and saved a nickel by not getting a cup of coffee. I had planned to live in New York for five months this time, which was the period in which I hoped to finish both first and second drafts of the new novel, but the book was going so slowly that more time than that would be necessary.

8.

I would have been much hungrier that autumn in New York if I had not been fortunate enough to have a meal given me several times a week during October and November. The room adjoining mine on the third floor was occupied by an interesting young woman who had two electric hot plates on which she prepared meals twice a day. Cooking was not permitted in the rooming house, but in this instance the landlord evidently had been lenient. Mouth-watering odors of food filled the hall and seeped through the crack under my door every afternoon.

A week after I had moved into the house, the girl told me that her name was Marianna and that she had come to New York from Miami early in September. She appeared to be about twenty-eight or twenty-nine years old—I was twenty-seven then—and she was small and brown-haired and evidently able to spend considerable money on her clothes. She did not go out to work.

Call It Experience

The first time I was invited to dinner was one evening about the middle of October while I was sitting in my room with the door partly open. I was eating bread and cheese. Marianna looked into my room and asked if that was all I was going to have for dinner.

I told her, truthfully but no doubt forlornly, that it was my usual meal at that time of day.

She immediately asked me to come to her room and eat some of the beef stew she had cooked. I had smelled the stew cooking for the past two hours and was hungrier than I had been before eating bread and cheese. I followed her into the next room and saw that she had already set a card table with two plates and cups and saucers. I drank the first coffee I had tasted in nearly a week.

While I was having a second cup of coffee, Marianna asked me how my first name was spelled. After I told her, she asked if anyone called me Skinny.

"Sometimes," I said. "How did you know?"

"Because that's the only logical diminutive of Erskine that I could imagine. It's from the last syllable of your name."

It probably was an appropriate nickname for another reason as well. Although I had weighed as much as a hundred and eighty pounds when I played football, during the past several lean years I had weighed as little as ninety-eight pounds and rarely more than a hundred and twenty-five. I was six feet tall.

She next asked me why I spent so much time writing on a typewriter and I told her that I was working on a novel. She said she had wanted to write short stories when she finished college, but instead had taught school for three years.

We sat there talking for about an hour and during that time I noticed that Marianna appeared to be nervous and apprehensive of something. Whenever there was a sound of footsteps in the hall or on the stairway, she listened intently as though expecting somebody. The door of the room had been locked.

"Is somebody else coming?" I asked her.

She shook her head quickly. "I don't think so," she answered. Then she said decidedly, "No. Nobody's coming."

Presently she got up and went to the window and looked through parted curtains. After watching the street below for several minutes, she came back and sat down.

"I'm afraid," she said then, trembling a little. Her face had become white and tense. "I really am."

"Afraid of what?" I asked, surprised.

She looked at me for a long time as though debating whether she would say anything more.

"Why don't you tell me?" I urged.

"There's a man—" She stopped and looked at me as if she had suddenly become mistrustful of every human being in the world. Several moments passed before another word was spoken. "—An awful man," she continued then. "He owns a restaurant near the corner, on Columbus Avenue. He's going to—I don't know what! But he threatens me—nearly every day."

"If somebody threatens you, why don't you tell the police? They'll help you."

"He told me not to."

"You could leave—go somewhere else. You could go back to Florida, couldn't you?"

She shook her head with a startled expression.

"Why can't you go back to Florida?" I asked her.

"Because he told me not to."

"How long have you known him?"

"Since I met him in Miami—a year ago."

"Did he tell you to come to New York?"

She nodded.

"Does he ever come here to see you?"

"No," she replied at once.

"When do you see him?"

"When I go to the restaurant."

"Stay away from there then."

"I can't. I don't know what's the matter with me. But I can't stay away from him. I couldn't keep from coming to New York when he told me to. I just had to do what he said. I don't know why I do what he tells me—but I have to. I don't know what's going to happen to me. But something will—and I'm so afraid!"

"What do you think he would do—if he did anything?"

"Beat me—and I don't know what else."

"What makes you think that?" I asked.

"I don't know," she said. "But I do—all the time."

Marianna got up then and began washing dishes in the bathroom. I got up and walked around the room, wondering about her. She appeared to be normal in every way except for her fear of somebody, real or imaginary. I could not decide whether she had made up the whole story or whether some man actually did have such power over her. When she finished washing the dishes, she changed her clothes in the bathroom and then came back and sat down on the studio bed.

Neither of us mentioned her fear again until I left at midnight to go back to my room.

"If anybody ever comes here," I said, "will you let me know?"

"He'll never come here," she answered solemnly, slowly shaking her head. "I have to go there. He told me to."

During the remainder of October and all of November, I went to Marianna's room several times a week and ate meals that she prepared, but she did not reveal anything more about her fear than she had the first time. She still insisted, however, that a man was going to harm her in some way and she continued to believe it was inevitable. She left the house only for a short time each day when she went out to buy food.

Early in December she went out one afternoon while snow was falling and did not come back. The landlord unlocked her door after three days and notified the police. Somewhere in the room they found the address of relatives in Miami and notified them that Marianna had disappeared. After about a week her belongings were packed and shipped to Florida.

The landlord told me afterward that the police had

questioned the owner of a small restaurant on Columbus Avenue and that he had told of seeing a girl of Marianna's description come into the restaurant several times during the past three months. He said he had never spoken to her, nor had she ever spoken to him, and he convinced the police that he did not know anything about her disappearance.

9.

The novel I was writing about a family living on an isolated back-road farm in Maine became progressively more difficult to manage during the remainder of the year and I was far from being satisfied with the first draft of it. The second draft, which I began in January and finished in March, 1932, was in my opinion a much better novel than the first draft had been. It was more readable and closer to the purpose I had in mind.

I went back to Mount Vernon in March to get the manuscript ready to submit to Charles Scribner's Sons. Under the terms of my contract, Scribner's had an option to publish the next two books I wrote after *Tobacco Road*.

In the meantime, *Tobacco Road* had been published in the month of February. The distribution of the novel was only slightly more brisk than the distribution of the volume of short stories had been and total sales were only a few thousand copies. The advance royalty was barely earned, which meant there was slight prospect of my receiving any money from it that year, and I could not keep from worrying about how I was going to be able to support my family. There were plenty of potatoes and rutabagas to eat, but that was about all.

Again Horace Gregory, William Soskin, Harry Emerson Wildes, James Gray, and a number of other critics wrote perceptive reviews; the proportion of dissenting reviews remained about the same. The reviews I saw were generally similar to those of the earlier book, although notices of the novel appeared in a larger number of newspapers and magazines and the space devoted to it in most publications was considerably larger.

My regard for the qualifications and intellectual honesty of the average reviewer undergoing no change, I did not allow myself to become overly elated by the favorable reviews, nor unduly depressed by the unfavorable ones. My mental attitude, following the publication of *Tobacco Road*, remained the same as it had been when I finished writing the book. It would have been next to impossible for anyone to convince me that the novel had not told a worthwhile story and that its conception of the life it depicted was not authentic.

It was nearly a month before Max Perkins said anything about the manuscript of the new novel I had sent him. He wrote then to say that the several readers at Scribner's had failed to reach complete agreement and that, although he was in favor of publishing it, he alone could not accept it under the circumstances. This was distressing news. Besides meaning that I would be unable to get an advance royalty payment on which to live, it was the first rejection I had received in a long time and overconfidence had left me unprepared for it. At first I was so discouraged and unhappy that I seriously considered giving up writing and turning to something else for a livelihood. I soon realized how ill advised this was, and after thinking it over for several days, I went to New York.

To my surprise, Max Lieber was by no means perturbed by what had happened. In fact, he maintained that it was a fortunate turn of events, saying that it placed him in a position to negotiate for more favorable terms with another publisher. He had talked to Max Perkins and had full knowledge of the divided opinion that had caused the rejection. After hearing his report, it was my understanding that Charles Scribner, Sr., whom I had never seen, disliked the novel and opposed its publication.

We went to see Max Perkins in his office and had a long friendly talk. In the end, Max Perkins said he hoped I would not want to seek another publisher but offer Scribner's my next book even though the rejection of the present novel voided the option clause of the contract and gave me the right to publish elsewhere.

I was willing to agree to the proposal, but by means of forceful diplomacy Max Lieber succeeded in getting me out of the office before my respect for Max Perkins's editorial judgment led me to commit myself. We left in a friendly spirit, saying it was a matter that Max Lieber and I needed time to consider, and went to a coffee shop and spent the next two hours trying to come to some decision.

"You're a free man," Max Lieber said finally. He was becoming provoked with me for not saying I would not return to Scribner's. "Skinny, there's no reason in the world why you shouldn't make the move that's going to be most beneficial for your own interests. An author has to have his books published, or he ceases to be an active author. I like this novel you've written, Max Perkins says he likes it, and you've said you like it. Isn't that the answer?"

"I don't know, Max," I told him. I was still unable to bring myself to the point of giving up my association with Max Perkins. "I just don't know what to do."

"Then look at it this way, Skinny. You've spent a good part of a year writing the book, and if you don't have it published, you'll have nothing to show for your work. Isn't it more sensible to go ahead with some other publisher than let sentimental reasons hold you to Scribner's? Be realistic in your thinking. You've got to look out for yourself in life. You've got a family to support, and your only source of income is from your writing. That's the down-to-earth economic side of it. I know how much regard you have for Max Perkins, both personally and as an editor, and I have similar respect for him, but he said himself that he thought the book should be published. You owe it to yourself to take the step."

"Who would publish it?" I asked.

"There're several enterprising publishers who would be eager to bring it out. Leave that to me."

"But that means leaving Scribner's."

"Naturally."

After knowing Max Perkins as long as I had, it was disturbing to think that such a decision would mean I would no longer be in a position to call upon him for help and advice. I had come to look forward to receiving letters from him, and when I found one in the mail, it was always the first to be read.

We left the coffee shop and walked back to Max Lieber's office. By the time we got there, I was ready to take his advice. When I told him so, he asked me to come back the following day. I walked up Fifth Avenue to the Scribner building and stood at the corner looking up at the windows of Max Perkins's office. After a while my eyes became blurred, and when I finally walked away, I was thinking of how I could tell Max Lieber that I had changed my mind and did not wish him to find another publisher.

When I reached Max Lieber's office the next morning, he enthusiastically told me there were only a few minutes in which to keep an appointment he had made with Harold Guinzburg and Marshall Best at The Viking Press. I wanted to stay there and explain to Max how I felt about leaving Scribner's, but he was so excited over the prospect of coming to an understanding with Viking that I was unable to bring myself to say anything.

Harold and Marshall were quick to point out the advantages to be gained by signing a contract with The Viking Press, and after an abundant and leisurely lunch, I was persuaded to submit my next three books to them.

Call It Experience

As we were leaving, Max handed Harold and Marshall the manuscript of the novel that had been rejected by Scribner's.

I went back to Mount Vernon as soon as the terms of the contract with Viking had been agreed upon. At first I regretted more than ever that I had given up my association with Max Perkins, but later I knew I was pleased with the interest shown by Harold Guinzburg and Marshall Best in my work.

After thinking about it for several days, I wondered if I had been influenced to change publishers by the fact that Harold and Marshall had taken me to lunch and urged me to eat all I could without regard to cost. The one and only time Max Perkins took me to lunch, he ordered for each of us a peanut butter and jelly sandwich and a glass of orange juice. The only comment I recall his making at the time was to the effect that in Vermont the lean and hungry countenance of man was held in fearsome respect.

I was asking myself now if I really wanted to have the Maine novel published at that time. It had served the purpose for which it had been written, it having been undertaken in an effort to clear my mind of the experience of writing *Tobacco Road*, and now I was certain I wanted to continue writing about the South. For the past several weeks I had been thinking of a story, which I felt could be written as forcefully as *Tobacco Road*, about another phase of life in East Georgia.

The decision was made for me. As it had happened at Scribner's, the editors at Viking did not agree in their opinion of the novel in manuscript; or perhaps they were unanimously opposed to its publication. Anyway, by that time I was certain I wanted the book put aside, and Max Lieber reluctantly withdrew his objection. As it was, I had not gained the principal objective by changing publishers, but I had come to be pleased with my new association. I was anxious to get to work at once on the next Southern novel, and it seemed probable that it would be finished in time to be published early the following year.

Early in May I began writing the novel I called *God's Little Acre*.

10.

Although I had made my home in Mount Vernon for several years, I had not yet written a book there. *American Earth* had been written for the most part in Augusta, Morgana, Baltimore, and Portland; *Tobacco Road* had been written in a room in the Fifties in New York; and the novel still in manuscript had been written in the West Eighties near Central Park.

It was necessary for me to come back to Mount Vernon for the summer to cut wood and raise potatoes and, besides, I did not have enough money to stay in New York or to go elsewhere. Though few little magazines made any payment at all, the five dollars or the ten dollars or the twenty-five dollars I sometimes received for a short story was the only available money for the household. Stories were appearing that year in *Pagany*, *Story*, *Clay*, *Contact*, *Contempo*, and *The New English Weekly*. One of these had been selected to be reprinted in *The Best Short Stories of 1932*. The title of this story was *Warm River* and it had been first published in *Pagany*, the quarterly edited by Richard Johns.

In the springtime warmth of May in Maine I was glad the time had come for me to write a book there. The long days were sometimes bright with sunshine, though more frequently misty in the climate of changeable Down East weather; and yet, whether the days were sunny or dull, they were usually balmy and pleasant. The woodchucks could be seen sunning themselves on the gray fieldstone walls and rabbits came at dusk to nibble on the dooryard lawn. The evenings were often chilly, but not so cold that fires were needed.

To the same extent that I liked the prospect of being able to write each succeeding book in a different place, I also liked to experiment each time with a different method of writing. Until now I had always written two or more drafts of every novel and novelette, and had rewritten and revised my short stories many times, and when I began *God's Little Acre*, I wanted the first draft to be such a finished novel that it would be ready for publication as soon as the last page was written. The story of *God's Little Acre* was so close to the surface of my consciousness, and the characters so familiar to my mind, that I was confident it could be accomplished in this manner. When the first page was written, I was certain it could be done that way. I took the sheet of paper from my typewriter, placed it upside down on the floor, and did not look at it again until the final page had been finished.

Since there was considerable physical labor to be done in the woodlot and vegetable garden that spring and summer, I decided to write indoors on the even days of the month and to work outdoors on the odd days. In this way equal time was devoted to the two tasks and I was able to accomplish what I wanted to both indoors and out. At the end of the first month, potatoes had been eyed and planted, two cords of beech and maple had been cut, and the pages of five chapters of the novel lay upside down on the floor.

After two months, a good two thirds of *God's Little Acre* had been put on paper. Even though I had not read any of it since it had come from the typewriter, I had a feeling of complete assurance and satisfaction about it.

Beginning early in July, guests began coming to Mount Vernon for the week end. Alfred Morang came up frequently from Portland and sat in the shade of an apple tree and painted all day. Another frequent visitor from Portland was a blue-eyed, fair-haired Scandinavian girl who liked to get up early in the morning to engage in calisthenics on the dewy lawn for half an hour before breakfast. This was only one phase of physical culture that she practiced; she also held sun-bathing in high esteem.

My next-door neighbor, Arthur Dolloff, walked over one afternoon to see what progress I was making in the woodlot and accidentally came upon Signe picking blackberries in a thicket on the hillside. After this brief, word-less encounter with her, he paused only long enough to inspect the canvas Alfred was working on and then hurried to where I was sawing in the woodlot.

"Notice you've got company from the city again," Arthur commented by way of greeting, making a slight motion with his chin toward the briar bushes and apple orchard fifty yards away.

I said something in reply without looking up from the log I was sawing.

"That painting fellow appears to be unharmful," he said. "Can't say it's useful, but it could tend to keep a man out of common mischief, as long as his mind won't wander." He turned and glanced in the direction of the blackberry bushes. "It's a sensible thing for a city-raised visitor to stay in the shade like he's doing. He won't be plagued with painful sunburn and blister if he keeps his head and stays where he's at."

Arthur made no further remarks until I had sawn through the maple log.

"Can't help but worry some about the young girl, though," he said gravely.

"Why, Arthur?" I asked him.

"Most peculiar way to gather berries I ever saw or heard tell. You should supply her with some cast-off clothing, if it's because she's wary of ripping and tearing her good city wear amongst the briars. Maybe you don't have the knowledge of it, if you've been tending to your sawing here in the woodlot, so I'll tell you. She's over there on that south slope above the orchard, plumb-square in the thick of the prickly briars, stripped out-and-out naked from head-top to big toe. Any man with common ableness should come close to hearing her skin scorch and sizzle in the hot sun."

"Signe's a physical culturist, Arthur," I explained. "Sun-bathing is one of her ideas about staying healthy. She's a nudist."

"Should say she is!" he said emphatically. "Only I wouldn't be one to call it by an out-of-the-way name. I'd speak right out in the common language and say she's just plain naked, the whole of her."

"She's a Scandinavian, Arthur. Many Scandinavians are great believers in some form of physical culture."

"Never had the will to learn much about the foreigners, but would guess their skin can take a blistering like any of the humans. If she's going to keep that up, and don't want to be seen wearing her clothing, you should step right in and assert yourself and caution her to heist an umbrella over her head. Being one of the city folks, she's going to get a painful case of blistering sunburn the way she is now."

Arthur remained silent after that until I had sawn another chunk of heater wood.

"Planning to stay here another year, after the present one?" he inquired pointedly.

"As long as I can pay the hundred dollars a year rent, or else find a thousand dollars to buy the place."

"If you're minded to stay, maybe you'll come around to getting in your firewood in the autumn and winter of the year, when the sap's down. If you made a move to do that, you wouldn't have to labor so hard sawing wet wood, and then having to dry it out, besides. Not many townsmen I know of would be caught sawing wood in the spring and summer, when the sap's up."

I thanked him for the advice, and then tried to explain that the reason I cut wood in the summer was because I was usually away from home in the fall and winter. He was not impressed by my explanation. He scooped up a handful of damp sawdust and squeezed it until it had been compressed into a hard moist cake. With a meaningful glance at me, he then tossed the sawdust aside.

"Planning to do any farming, if you stay here?" he asked after a while.

"Only enough to grow potatoes and rutabagas in the garden," I told him. "I have to spend the rest of the time writing. Writing is my trade, Arthur."

There was a long pause, and I knew before he spoke again that he had found the opportunity he had been seeking. He had never forgotten the time in midwinter when the rats moved from the bitter cold of my house to the warmth of his, and he had to retaliate in some way before he would have peace of mind.

"Writer by trade," he said with a short nod. "Don't make much of a decent living following it, do you?"

"I'm afraid I haven't, so far," I admitted.

Saying nothing more, and obviously satisfied, Arthur went down through the woodlot in the opposite direction from which he had come, avoiding the blackberry thicket on the sunny slope above the apple orchard.

I I.

The writing of the final page, the final paragraph, the final sentence, and then the last word of *God's Little Acre* was the most satisfying experience I had had since I first began writing. I was far more pleased with what I had done than I had been when I finished writing *Tobacco Road*. For one thing, the novel covered a broader scene and brought into a single story the way of life in a Southern mill town and the everyday existence of a family on a farm. I had started the new novel with confidence and without the fears and uncertainties about its outcome that had bothered me throughout the writing of the earlier novel. Now I felt for the first time in my life that I could consider myself a professional novelist.

The book was finished late in August, and a few days later I took it to New York. Everyone at The Viking Press seemed to be surprised to hear that I had come with the completed manuscript of a new novel, and even Max Lieber was surprised when he saw it. When it was given to Harold Guinzburg and Marshall Best, they were not immediately convinced that I had written it during the past three months.

It was my intention to stay in New York until Harold and Marshall read the manuscript and came to a decision about it, but I was less able financially to pay hotel expenses this time than I had been on previous trips. When

Marshall heard of this, he asked me to stay with him at his apartment.

A few days later the novel was accepted and scheduled for publication in the early spring of 1933, and Max arranged for an advance royalty payment that amounted to twice as much as I had ever before received for a book. My gross income for 1932 totaled almost seven hundred dollars, the largest yearly sum I had received from writing. I went back to Maine and paid a year's rent in advance and had enough money left over to support my family for the next six months. We had beef roast and steak for the first time in nearly a year. The rutabagas were left to rot in the ground that fall; I hoped I had eaten the last one of the yellow roots I would have to swallow as long as I lived.

Max Lieber had sent me several papers and agreements to sign during the past year and, since I was so deeply interested in what I was writing and had little interest in the business details connected with my work, I had given slight attention to these things. One of the agreements I had signed, I was reminded at this time in a letter from Max, had granted Jack Kirkland the right to dramatize *Tobacco Road* for the stage, and now Jack was asking that the option be extended. The theater was so remote from my life that I had given the matter of a dramatization little thought; it still seemed unlikely that anyone would actually adapt a novel of mine for the stage. I wrote Max that I was not particularly interested in the matter, but that if he insisted I would sign the extension. Max assured me that Jack Kirkland was seriously interested in making a play of *Tobacco Road* and intended to have it produced on Broadway. I signed the paper and mailed it without comment to Max.

What interested me more than anything else then was the writing of short stories. I had devoted most of the time during the past two years to the writing of three novels, and most of the stories I had written previously were either already in print or had been accepted for publication.

I went to work that fall in an upstairs room of the big house and wrote one story after another. It did not occur to me to ask myself what my purpose was in writing short stories and novels until the question was put to me with increasing frequency. I liked writing fiction as some men liked raising cattle or playing baseball or practicing law, and, because I was unhappy doing anything else, I wanted to make it my vocation. And at the same time I wanted to succeed in my field, and to earn my living, just as if it had been any other profession or trade that men live by. When I was asked why I wrote fiction, I could only say that I liked to write; when I was asked to explain the meaning of a story or novel, I could only say that it meant what it said to the reader. I had no philosophical truths to dispense, no evangelistic urge to change the course of human destiny. All I wanted to do was simply to describe to the best of my ability the aspirations and despair of the people I wrote about. If there were lessons to be learned therein, they were to be found in these descriptions of life, and each reader, according to his own conscience, was free to place his interpretation upon them.

Instead of submitting my work directly to magazines as I had in the past, I was now sending Max Lieber everything I wrote. He had been firm in his insistence that I stop giving away short stories to little magazines in order to find publication and got me to agree to let him hold the stories even if they could not be placed immediately. Gradually, and one by one, they began appearing in magazines in which my work had not been previously published.

I was now able to buy a new Corona typewriter. The old typewriter, which had been in use for about ten years, was actually falling apart and the cost of repairing it was estimated to be close to the cost of a new machine. The dealer from whom I bought the new portable solemnly declared that the old one was beyond repair but finally allowed five dollars' credit for it.

The only extravagance I indulged in was the buying of three new copies of *Webster's Collegiate Dictionary*. One new copy would have been adequate, but for a long time it had been my ambition to have three dictionaries at the same time. The old, much-used dictionary, which I had carried everywhere I had been for the past dozen years, was coming to pieces and a number of pages were already missing. I put one new copy in the upstairs room where I worked, another in the living room, and the third copy in the kitchen. Wherever I happened to be in the house after that, I was always able to reach a dictionary quickly.

Call It Experience

Of my three most prized material possessions—typewriter, cigarette-making machine, and dictionary—I valued the dictionary by far the highest and would have certainly endeavored to hold on to it the longest. I not only consulted it frequently, but in my free time I read the dictionary instead of reading novels and magazines; in my estimation, nothing had been written that was as fascinating, provocative, instructive, and fully satisfying as a book of words and their alluring meanings.

12.

Beginning early in February and ending in mid-December, 1933, was a crowded and eventful year. For the first time in almost a decade I did not write a single short story or novel during a twelve-month period. At the end of that time, however, I had learned what I considered a useful lesson: a writer should set aside ample time for the practice of his profession and guard it zealously, for otherwise he would find that many of his days had been given to exciting but unfruitful exploits. Having learned this truth, I was then able to view my experiences as having been a fortunate period in which to look backward to where I had come from and to look forward to where I wanted next to go.

At the start of the year, Marshall Best had suggested that I select a number of short stories for a volume that Viking wished to bring out. I chose twenty stories, most of them having been published during the past few months or which were scheduled to be published that year in *Esquire, Folk-Say, Pagany, Story, The New English Weekly,* and *The Yale Review.* I considered several possible titles, and finally decided to call the book *We Are the Living.* The manuscript was typed and taken to Marshall when I went to New York for the publication of *God's Little Acre.* Viking scheduled the volume of stories for publication in the fall of the year.

The publication of *God's Little Acre* brought forth as large a number of reviews as the two previous books combined had attracted. The proportion of favorable and unfavorable notices was about the same as it had been in the past. Among those who wrote comment at this time were Alexander Woollcott, Lewis Gannett, John Cowper Powys, Harry Hansen, Compton Mackenzie, Marc Connelly, and Joseph Henry Jackson. The circulation of *God's Little Acre,* which amounted to approximately ten thousand copies during its first season, was twice as large as the circulation of *Tobacco Road* had been.

I was staying with Marshall Best again. We went one evening to Harold Guinzburg's home and there I met Alexander Woollcott. It was my first encounter with Alec and I was awed both by his sharp wit and by his ponderous body. Not being a tall man, he looked rolypoly fat. He filled a chair to overflowing and, of course, stridently dominated the conversation. When Marshall and I were leaving, Alec asked me to come to see him at his apartment the next afternoon at five o'clock.

Call It Experience

I arrived at the address on time the next day and was shown by a servant to a small reception room. There I waited half an hour, and when Alec still had not appeared, I got up and walked restlessly around the apartment wondering if I had made a mistake about the day or time. A quarter of an hour later he opened a door partly and peered at me as though he had discovered an unwanted and undesirable guest.

"Your name's Caldwell," he said. "Did I ask you to come here?"

I nodded uncertainly.

The door was opened a few inches more.

"Why did I ask you?" he said.

"I don't know," I answered, quaking a little.

The door was thrown open. "Neither do I. Good-by!"

I backed across the room wondering if there was anything I could say under the circumstances. I knew I was on the verge of becoming angry, but I tried to keep from speaking up to a man of his age.

"There's the door behind you," he called out, pointing to it. He then came as far as the middle of the room and I saw for the first time that he was wearing a figured brocade robe in a shade of deep red. He looked like a fleshy, elderly woman in a Mother Hubbard. "Why don't you say something or do something?" he spoke up sharply. "What's the matter with you?"

"If you didn't look like somebody's grandmother, I would say something." I could feel anger coming over me and it was the first thought that came to mind.

"What's that?" he asked, raising his voice. His face

had brightened and his skin flushed to a reddish glow.
"What did you say, Caldwell? How was that?"

"You look too much like somebody's grandmother
for me to say it."

"Come back here!" he commanded, his short fat arms
waving and his delicately formed features glowing redly.
"Let's sit down and have a drink. I didn't think you'd
have either the spunk or the presence of mind to say
anything like that. A lot of people brighter than you are
frightened out of their wits by what is sometimes re-
ferred to as my biting sarcasm. I'm glad you're not—
but why aren't you?"

"I guess it's because I'm not familiar enough with
your reputation."

Chuckling a little, Alec rang for his servant. "I'm
having something civilized—brandy. What'll you have,
Caldwell? Something obnoxious like a martini?"

I stayed another half an hour and then left. When
I got back to Marshall Best's apartment and told him of
my encounter with Alec Woollcott, he looked relieved.
His only comment then was to say that I had got off
much more lightly than many of Alec's visitors.

Not long after the publication of *God's Little Acre*,
and it was then early in May, the novel was taken into
court on a charge of obscenity instituted by The New
York Society for the Suppression of Vice. The charge
was made by the Society's secretary, John S. Sumner,
and it was defended by The Viking Press. Among the
half a hundred critics and writers who came to the support of the novel, Alexander Woollcott was one of the

many who spoke out loudly in its behalf. Three weeks later the charge was dismissed by Magistrate Benjamin E. Greenspan in a written opinion in which he found the book not obscene. Magistrate Greenspan's opinion was printed in subsequent editions of *God's Little Acre*.

13.

At the end of May, 1933, a few days after the charge against *God's Little Acre* in New York had been dismissed, I was some sixty miles south of New Orleans fighting mosquitoes day and night in a shrimp fisherman's shanty built on stilts over the marshes of Barataria Bay. I was a junior screenwriter with a Metro-Goldwyn-Mayer motion picture production unit on location, and the reason for my being there was because Max Lieber, along with Leland Hayward, also an agent at the time, knew that I had spent my last dollar to come to New York to attend court proceedings, and they both felt that it was desirable to do something to improve my financial condition.

Metro-Goldwyn-Mayer had been seeking a writer to help with the writing of a screenplay for a picture which Todd Browning was to direct, and Max and Leland decided that I should have the assignment. The three-month contract called for a salary of two hundred and fifty dollars weekly, but it was not until I had drawn my second week's salary that I was fully convinced that such a sum of money would be paid once a week and not once a month.

Shaky on my feet, without food since the previous afternoon, I had arrived in New Orleans, on a sputtering three-engine plane of a pioneering airline, after losing an argument with M-G-M. It had seemed to me that the most logical way to travel from New York to New Orleans was to take a fast Southern Railway train in the afternoon which would arrive in New Orleans the following night. It was a train trip of about thirty hours. Besides, I had never been on an airplane and I saw no good reason why I should have to suffer my first flight at that time.

It had been M-G-M's inflexible plan that I should take an evening train on the New York Central System to Cleveland, get off there, and board an American Airways (the name of the company was later changed to American Airlines) plane for New Orleans. When I pointed out that this method of travel would require about thirty hours, the same as a Southern Railway train all the way, I was informed that commercial passenger aviation in the United States was struggling to establish itself and that M-G-M, being a progressive organization, had made it a policy to provide aviation with all possible encouragement; and, additionally, that since the motion-picture studio was paying my fare and incidental expenses, I could do no less than gracefully co-operate to the fullest extent.

I took the night train to Cleveland. Just before the

train left Grand Central Station, I was told that a representative of the airline would come aboard the train at a Cleveland surburb at five-thirty a.m., wake me up, and see to it that I got off the train and was taken to the airport. The final detail was that I would be served a complimentary hot breakfast before boarding the plane.

As it happened, nobody had got on the train to wake me up; however, I woke up shortly before six o'clock, barely in time to get dressed and get off the train when it stopped in Cleveland. Nobody at the station seemed to know anything about the situation, so I took a taxi to the airport. The taxi driver told me along the way that the passenger-waking service, as well as the hot breakfasts, had been discontinued by the airline the week before. I arrived in New Orleans fourteen bumpy, wretchedly airsick hours later; the train I had wanted to take the previous afternoon in New York arrived at approximately the same time.

In New Orleans I stayed at the Roosevelt Hotel for several days waiting for transportation to Barataria Bay, and then one morning I was put aboard a barge and taken down a bayou to a marshy inlet on the Gulf of Mexico. I lived in a screenless shanty on a shrimp platform and sat in it most of the time wrapped in mosquito nets watching the Japanese shrimp fishermen dry their catches on the platform, and waiting to be told what was expected of me as a screenwriter.

Howard Wallace, one of the other writers on location, said he had a fairly clear idea of what the story was about, but that the story-line had been changed several times recently, both in Hollywood and on location, and he was not sure just what would be done with it. As closely as I could come to comprehending it, the story had to do in some manner with the beautiful young daughter of a Cajun muskrat trapper who drowned herself in a hyacinth-clogged bayou as the consequence of disappointment in love.

We stayed for about a week on the shrimp platform, expecting Todd Browning to decide any day just how the story was going to be told on the screen, but Todd was deeply engrossed with the problems of photographing background scenery for process footage. Howard told me not to worry, explaining that motion pictures were nearly always finished somehow; besides, he said, it was a good opportunity to learn how to adjust myself to the way of life in the motion-picture industry. I admitted that so far it did seem to differ from the life with which I was familiar, and that I was somewhat confused.

After a week, Howard and I were taken to New Orleans and put aboard the Sunset Limited of the Southern Pacific Railroad with tickets to Los Angeles. The others in the location unit remained at Barataria Bay to do more shooting for process scenes.

We each had been furnished with lower-berth accommodations by the studio. I was satisfied with my lower berth, which was an improvement over a seat in a jolting bus, but Howard took the attitude that the studio should have provided superior accommodations for its screenwriters. He became very unhappy and spoke of the loss of face.

Call It Experience

We were to spend two days and three nights on the Sunset Limited, and after the first night in our lower berths, Howard had made up his mind to do something about it. He said we would take a drawing room, pay the difference ourselves, and demand that the studio refund the amount to us when we got to California. Howard was an experienced Hollywood screenwriter, and I was merely a junior one without experience, so I agreed. We moved into a drawing room.

It so happened that Howard had seen a young woman on the train with whom he thought he should be acquainted, and he invited her to sit in our drawing room. In the late afternoon the drawing room became stuffy and crowded, and it was suggested that I would have more leg room and be more comfortable in general in the young woman's space in the next car.

When I returned from the diner that evening, I could not find Howard, and the drawing-room door was locked. However, my baggage had been moved to the next car, and I spent the next two nights in an upper berth. It provided a good opportunity for me to meditate on the way of life in the motion-picture industry. Howard explained the situation by saying that he had decided I would have more time to think about the screen story in the privacy of an upper berth, and he offered to give me back my share of the additional money we had paid for the superior Pullman accommodations.

14.

A studio limousine met us early in the morning at the Alhambra Station. Howard Wallace got out at his home in Beverly Hills and I went to the Metro-Goldwyn-Mayer studio in Culver City. The receptionist at the studio entrance, looking surprised and saying it was unusually early for a screenwriter to be coming to work, suggested that I go away somewhere and come back at about ten o'clock.

On the way to the studio I had noticed the Culver City Hotel, the tallest building in the neighborhood; I picked up my suitcase and typewriter and walked up the street several blocks to it and engaged a room. The weekly rate was somewhat higher than I had paid at the Warwick Hotel in Hollywood, but, since I had no automobile and no intention of buying one, I had planned to live within walking distance of the studio and the cost of the room was modest enough. As I walked through the lobby of the hotel, I did not see anyone who looked as if he were a writer, but there were numerous men and women who had the appearance of actors and performers. Some were midgets, some had the robust physique of acrobats, and many were dressed in gaudy cowboy garb.

At ten o'clock I walked down Washington Boulevard to the M-G-M studio. After waiting three-quarters of an hour, I was taken into a large, richly carpeted room containing a number of leather upholstered couches,

143

overstuffed divans, deep-seated chairs, and over-size ash-trays that looked like flower pots. It was a bright, sunny day outside, but the Venetian blinds were closed tightly over the windows and the room was dimly illuminated by softly tinted concealed lights. There were several producers, associate producers, and assistant producers in various relaxed postures about the room. After I had been introduced, a man in one of the deep-seated chairs asked in a startlingly enthusiastic manner what I thought of the picture I had been working on.

"Don't ask me," I said right away. "I probably know less about it than anybody here."

Producers, associates, and assistants looked at me as though I had insulted each of them personally.

"What do you mean by that, Caldwell?" somebody asked presently.

"I didn't see anybody in Louisiana who knew anything about the story. A good-looking Cajun girl is going to drown herself in a hyacinth bayou—and that's all I know about it so far."

"Motivation, man!" somebody shouted excitedly. "Give us motivation! That's what we've been waiting for!"

There was a deep silence in the room after that for several moments.

"And you mean you haven't finished the script?" somebody else asked in a calmer voice.

"No," I said. "I haven't written anything yet. I want to know more about the story first."

There was a hurried conference among the producers

in a far corner of the large office, and when it was over, somebody took me by the arm and asked me to step outside and wait in the reception room. Half an hour later one of the two secretaries came over and asked me where I was living. I told her I was staying at the Culver City Hotel. She looked startled for a moment before making a note of it on her pad. Then she said I was to go to see Sam Marx.

Sam Marx was a story editor and a man with a personality well adapted to dealing diplomatically with the awkward situations that sometimes suddenly arose between producers and writers. Sam took me to lunch and afterward consulted me on the choice of a room in the writers' building. After some words of friendly advice, he pointed out the crying-towel hanging beside the bulletin board and then left me to become adjusted to the life of a junior screenwriter on the M-G-M lot.

Several days later, Sam came to tell me that the story I had come to work on had been put on the shelf temporarily and suggested that I might like to work on other studio story material. He took me to a sound stage where the studio was having story trouble with a Miriam Hopkins picture. The problem, as I saw it, was merely to give Miriam something to do in greeting her lover when he arrived. The solution seemed simple enough to me. I proposed that she get up, walk gracefully to him, and have him take her in his arms. I was quickly reminded by a producer's supervisor that we were living in the age of talking pictures, not silent ones, and that a screenwriter should provide dialogue for any situation. Another writer was sent for, and when I left, Miriam was wearily swinging on the porch in her summery frock and her lover was still sitting on a stool nearby reading *Variety*.

Sam told me that M-G-M was planning a series of short features based on F.B.I. files to be called *Crime Does Not Pay*, and I was offered several of the stories for screen treatment. The first one I selected had the title of *The Express Train Robbery*.

After I had been in Culver City for two weeks, Jack Kirkland phoned me at the hotel one Sunday and asked me to come down to Leland Hayward's beach house at Santa Monica. I wanted to go, but as I had no car, nor any idea how long it would take me to get there on a bus, I declined. Later, Jack told me that the dramatization he had been writing was finished and that he expected to have *Tobacco Road* on Broadway in the fall.

On Saturdays I took the long bus trip to Hollywood and got into the habit of going to Stanley Rose's Bookshop on Hollywood Boulevard. Stanley Rose's was a popular gathering place for an assorted and argumentative group of writers, would-be writers, and infrequent book buyers. According to Stanley, an insignificant number of books were sold there, but the bookshop, and especially the back room, was usually crowded afternoon and evening. When Stanley had to sell some books in order to keep his business going and to pay rent and the electric-light bill, he no longer attempted to persuade one of the conversationalists in the shop to buy one, but instead filled several bags full of books and peddled them at the motion-picture studios.

Call It Experience

Shortly before I left California to return to Maine, Stanley sent out invitations to a Saturday-evening cocktail party in his bookshop. The party was to begin at eight o'clock, but by seven the small shop was already filled with a hundred or more persons, most of whom were uninvited but none the less enthusiastic guests. When the invited guests arrived at eight o'clock, many of them could not get into the crowded bookshop but had to stand on the sidewalk and look through the windows.

Stanley had told me in advance that creditors were hounding him, that he was desperately in need of trade in order to remain in business, and that the only purpose of the party was to prevail upon a young woman, who had recently started writing a Hollywood newspaper column, to make favorable mention of his bookshop and thereby attract needed customers. The strikingly attired young woman was Hedda Hopper, and when I was introduced to her, I forget all about Stanley's urgent plea that I persuade her to write something helpful about his bookshop.

When I did remember what I was expected to do, we had become separated in the crowded back room and I could not get anywhere near Hedda again. As she was leaving, I called to her above the din of conversation.

"I'll remember you by your hat, even if I didn't get to talk to you."

"If you enjoy my hats, that's all that matters," she said as she pushed through the crowd and left.

Toward midnight, when only a handful of guests remained, Stanley took me aside and anxiously asked what I had said to Hedda about his bookshop.

I apologized the best I could. "Stanley, I tried to get to Hedda and talk about it, but there was too much of a crowd here. I just didn't have a chance."

"You mean you didn't say anything at all to her—you didn't get her to promise to write up my bookshop?"

"I didn't get to say anything about your bookshop, Stanley, but I thought she had on a funny-looking hat, and I told her so."

"This's going to ruin me," he said accusingly. "Now she'll go and write a whole column about what somebody said about her hats—and not a penny's worth about my bookshop. After I'd gone and spent hard-to-get seventy-five dollars on this party, just to get Hedda to write it up, you went and took her mind off of it. I wish you'd had the sense not to mention hats while Hedda Hopper was anywhere around."

"But, anyway, Stanley," I said, "you sold a lot of books here tonight, didn't you? That'll be a help."

"Sold books to the intelligentsia?" he said gloomily. "All that crowd ever does is listen to themselves talk. They think only peasants buy books."

15.

The first week in September I was back in Mount Vernon with twenty-five hundred dollars of the money I had earned during the past three months. Ten per cent of my salary had gone to Max Lieber and Leland Hayward for agency commission, I had lived on twenty-five dollars a week in California, and I had spent a hundred dollars for clothing and incidentals.

After Labor Day I went to Portland and paid off the thousand-dollar note at the bank, and then I bought a new Ford, the first automobile I had ever owned that was not secondhand when I acquired it. This depleted my funds considerably, but in a few days I received notification, together with a check for one thousand dollars, that I had been given *The Yale Review's* 1933 award for fiction. This windfall made it possible for me to buy the house in Mount Vernon for my family; and I did so at once, paying one thousand dollars in cash for it. The title of the short story, which had been published in *The Yale Review* that spring, was *Country Full of Swedes*. Before that, the story had had a dismal experience of rejection; for a year it had been turned down in rapid succession by a dozen or more magazine editors. Shortly before it was accepted by *The Yale Review* it had been returned by the editor of another magazine with a discouraging note saying, "This old nag will never reach the post."

The Viking Press published *We Are the Living* that season, and Marshall Best said that they would like to have a new novel for the coming year. I had not written a line of fiction during the past nine months, and I did not even have a sufficient number of short stories to make another book. I told Marshall that I planned to begin writing again in January.

Casting and rehearsals of *Tobacco Road*, the play, began in November, and Anthony Brown, who was directing it, asked me to come to New York for several days. I attended several rehearsals, but had few suggestions to offer other than a strong insistence on the use of authentic dialect by the cast. I had read Jack Kirkland's script of the play, and had approved it, and he had followed the novel so closely that I saw no need for any changes.

Before leaving New York, I was taken to "21," a speakeasy in West Fifty-second Street, for the first newspaper interview I had ever given. The paper in which the interview appeared was *The New York Herald Tribune*, and when I read it the next day, I found that I was supposed to have made some surprising comments on life in the South and Down East. The comments I had made in contrasting life in the two regions, even when read in the light of a new day, still seemed normal and matter-of-fact to me.

Tobacco Road, the play, opened at the Masque Theatre in New York on Monday evening December 4, 1933, the date of the repeal of prohibition in the United States. It was produced by Jack Kirkland and Harry Oshrin, who were the sole owners of the production. My only financial interest in the play amounted to one half of the authors' royalty; Jack received also one half.

The reviews of the play, while similar to those of the novel, were not looked upon as being sufficiently favorable for Broadway, and it was generally believed that the production would have a life of only one or two weeks. However, operating expenses of the production were approximately twenty-five hundred dollars weekly and Jack and Harry believed the weekly overhead could be met. The play struggled along for two months with a weekly box-office gross of between two thousand and three thousand dollars. Although few plays had survived on Broadway for any length of time with so little money passing through the box office, Jack and Harry would not admit that it was a failure.

Then, in January, 1934, Captain Joseph M. Patterson, editor of *The Daily News*, published a series of editorials praising the play and urging readers to attend it. Box-office receipts doubled immediately and the gross continued to increase during the remainder of the season.

By the end of the first year, the play had become an established institution on Broadway, and when it finally closed, it had had a continuous run in New York of seven and a half years, setting a record for being at that time the play with the longest run in the history of the New York theater. Aside from any merits of the play itself, I attributed its success equally to Captain Patterson's editorials, to the acting of Henry Hull, who created the role of Jeeter Lester, and to Sam Byrd, who played the part of Dude. However, it is doubtful if any of these persons would have had an opportunity to contribute to the play's eventual success if it had not been for Jack Kirkland's determination to keep the play from closing when box-office receipts dropped below the break-even figure. In order to provide cash for theater rent, actors' salaries, and promotion expense, Jack took motion-picture writing assignments in Hollywood. He never admitted how much money he contributed in this manner, but it was considerable.

It was probably inevitable, because of many different casts which presented the play, that *Tobacco Road* had various interpretations from year to year. Some of these interpretations were serious, which I approved, and some were humorous, which I regretted. I always felt that the Henry Hull interpretation was the authentic and desirable one.

In addition to the original New York production, there were at various times two road companies of the play on tour in the United States. My one-half share of the authors' royalty for seven and a half years was as low as thirty-five dollars and as high as two thousand dollars weekly. Beginning in 1933 and continuing almost without interruption for the next seventeen years, *Tobacco Road*, the play, was staged somewhere in the United States or abroad by one or more acting companies.

Authorized, and unauthorized, foreign productions were staged in Argentina, Australia, Belgium, Brazil, Czechoslovakia, Denmark, England, Finland, France, Greece, Hungary, Italy, Norway, Sweden, and Switzerland. The longest runs abroad were in France, in 1948-49, and in England, in 1949-50; each of those two companies played more than a year's time.

In 1934 The Viking Press published Jack Kirkland's dramatization in book form. The motion-picture version of *Tobacco Road*, an inadequate screen presentation of either the novel or the play, was written by Nunnally

Johnson and produced by Twentieth Century–Fox Film
Corporation in 1941.

16.

My steadfast New Year's resolution, in 1934, was to
return to writing books without delay. A twelve-month
leave from the confining and exacting requirements of
authorship had been pleasant and profitable while it
lasted, but it had been spent far afield and now I was
dissatisfied and miserable. Debts had been paid off, a
house and automobile had been bought, I had done considerable traveling, enough money for a year's living
expenses had been put aside—all taking place in 1933—
but none the less I had failed to write a book for publication in 1934. As it seemed to me then, the sum of all these
accomplishments was of little worth in comparison with
the greater value to be had by writing and publishing
a book.

The full realization of failure at this point in my
scheme of living-to-write brought about such an unhappy
state of mind that I set out at once, the first week in January, to get some writing done. And as usual in recent
years, I left home to write. I became disagreeable, morose,
short-tempered, and unreasonably moody at such times,
and it was asking too much of my family to endure me
through such spells. I went to New York and rented, at
a weekly rate of seven dollars, a basement room in a
brownstone front in the West Eighties near Central

Park and began writing short stories from early morning until late in the night.

It was a bitterly cold winter in New York that year—it felt so to me in the damp basement room with an uncarpeted cement floor—and I was colder than I remembered ever having been in the State of Maine. I had become accustomed to stretching out flat on my back on the floor for twenty or thirty minutes after a long day sitting at the typewriter, and the cold and dampness of the basement room brought back twinges of chilblains in my hands. After a week of futile argument with the janitor about the lack of adequate heat in the room, I began taking bus trips for several days at a time.

A heated Greyhound bus was comfortably warm during the day. On smooth stretches of highway in the open country I wrote with pencil and pad, and at night I stopped at a hotel and wrote on a typewriter. Such trips, once or twice a week, were taken to Philadelphia, Baltimore, Washington, Scranton, Pittsburgh, Cleveland, Chicago, Detroit, and Buffalo.

At the end of six weeks—it was mid-February then—half a dozen satisfactory stories had been completed. One of these was a short novelette or long story called *Kneel to the Rising Sun*. This was a story about the injustice of a Southern landowner in dealing with one of his white tenants, a story which I had felt the need to write for several months, but it had been necessary to wait until there was ample time for such a lengthy work of fiction. It was rejected by numerous magazines for a year before it was accepted by Max Perkins and published in *Scribner's Magazine*. *Kneel to the Rising Sun* became the title story of a collection which The Viking Press issued the following year.

I returned to Mount Vernon in February with the confident knowledge that I would be able to keep warmer there than I had in the watery basement in New York and immediately began writing a novel in front of a glowing Franklin heater in the cottage on frozen, snow-hummocked Parker Lake.

The title of the novel I was writing was *Journeyman*. It was the story of an itinerant minister, unordained, in the rural South, who practiced roguery in the guise of his calling. I had observed his counterpart in life many times in Georgia, Florida, and the Carolinas and the idea on which the story was based had been in mind most of the past year. It was ready to be put down on paper as fast as I could type. I looked upon it as being one of the indigenous phases of life in the South which I wanted to include in a series of novels.

The only untoward interruption that took place during the writing of *Journeyman* was caused by the notification that it was necessary for me to file state and federal income-tax returns for the preceding year. It was the first time in my life that I had earned enough money to call for the payment of income tax in any amount and I was dismayed to find that I owed several hundred dollars.

The payment of this obligation all but did away with the fund I had put aside for living expenses during 1934. It was true that I was then receiving weekly royalty checks from *Tobacco Road*, the play, for various sums between fifty and seventy-five dollars, but the play was running on a week-to-week basis and to me it still seemed unlikely that the production would continue much longer. In addition, royalty currently being earned on published books was still being applied to repayment of advance royalty that already had been spent.

The novel was finished about the middle of May and sent to Harold Guinzburg and Marshall Best for consideration. While waiting to hear what was thought of *Journeyman* at Viking, I spent a good part of the time worrying about finding ways and means to support my family for the remainder of the year. I had only two hundred dollars at the time for that purpose; it was an amount that would provide for a budget of about twenty-five dollars monthly for a family of five persons.

17.

Long before any word was received from Viking as to whether or not *Journeyman* would be accepted and published, there was an unexpected communication from Metro-Goldwyn-Mayer asking me to return to California to work on screen stories at the Culver City studio. I consulted Max Lieber about the offer and, since M-G-M had proposed doubling my previous salary to amount to five hundred dollars weekly, it was decided that I should go for three months and thereby improve my financial muddle. I arrived in Los Angeles at the end of May.

Call It Experience

I spent several weeks reading screen material and writing and revising scenes for a number of partly completed scripts, and then Harry Behn, who had been a screenwriter for several years, suggested that we collaborate on an original screen story for the studio. This proposal was acceptable to Sam Marx and others concerned, and Harry and I moved to adjoining rooms in the writers' building. It was my first experience in collaborating with a screenwriter or with anyone else. I had never dictated a story, and Harry preferred dictation. It was decided that Harry would dictate one scene at a time and then I would revise the script before we went to the next scene.

We had agreed on the writing of a story about logging in the Northwest. The foreman of the logging camp was the hero and the daughter of a woodsman was the heroine. We made good progress with the story for the first two weeks; then suddenly we found ourselves in an atmosphere of complete blankness.

Harry Behn, who was tall and lithe and sinewy, had a habit of lying on one of the couches and twisting his arms, legs, and torso into pretzel-shaped positions while thinking and dictating. He seemed to be able to do his best work while his supple body was in contortions.

We had reached a point in a new scene where nothing we could devise seemed logical as the next step. On the couch, Harry's rubbery limbs were tied in a knot. Not a word had been dictated for the past quarter-hour. I was gazing out the window at a group of extras on an outdoor set and the stenographer was quietly turning the pages of a magazine. Suddenly Harry groaned.

"I'm stuck!" he yelled a moment later. "I can't do it! Get me out of here!"

The stenographer put down her magazine and I got up and walked across the room and back again. Harry's outburst had not sounded particularly unusual under the circumstances.

"Don't worry, Harry," I said sympathetically. "I think we'll be able to get this scene done right. Maybe we ought to quit for the day and start again fresh in the morning."

"I don't mean that!" he said in an agonized voice. "It's not the story—it's me! Something's wrong! I can't get untangled—I've got cramps in both legs!"

I went to the couch and looked down at Harry. He had crossed his legs behind his knees in such a manner that one of his arms was gripped so tightly in a leg-lock that his hand had become pale and bloodless for lack of circulation. His contorted position looked similar to a painful wrestling hold used by professionals in the ring. I tried to pull one of his feet free in order to break the lock, but Harry yelled at the top of his voice. He was in great pain.

"What should I do, Harry?" I asked him.

"I don't know, but do something quick—this's killing me! Hurry!"

A secretary in one of the nearby offices heard Harry yell, and she ran into the room. She was a small girl, frail in appearance. When she saw what had happened, she knelt on the floor beside the couch.

"That looks like a Boston crab hold you've got on

yourself, Mr. Behn," she said. "But how did you get an arm-lock, too?"

"I don't know," Harry said weakly. "But do something—quick!"

"I think I can release it," she told him. "Now, just be calm, Mr. Behn. I'm not going to hurt you."

First she pressed against one of his knees and then she deftly twisted a foot. Both of Harry's feet shot straight forward with a cracking sound in his knee joints and his arm fell limply from his shoulder. His left hand was deathly white. Perspiration covered his face.

"How did you know what to do?" I asked the girl while she was briskly rubbing Harry's hand and arm to restore circulation.

"I go to the wrestling matches every Wednesday night," she said, "and I've watched the referee untie holds like that many times. Who put the lock on Mr. Behn?"

"He did it to himself," I told her.

"That's quite an accomplishment for a screenwriter," she said with admiration. "Down at the wrestling matches it always takes a strong gorilla to tie up somebody like that."

My contract came to an end shortly after that and I left California. Harry Behn moved to Arizona. The logging story was never filmed.

18.

For many years I had looked forward to the time when I would have the opportunity to travel at leisure through America by automobile, going where I wished and stopping when I pleased, and when I left California in the late summer of 1934, the time at last was at hand.

I drove from state to state in the West, making a zig-zag pattern of the route traveled from the Pacific Coast to the Mississippi River. Sometimes driving twenty or thirty miles a day, sometimes two or three hundred, but never by prearranged plan, I knew long before the trip was finished that I wanted to write about some of the things that interested me along the way. The Viking Press had scheduled the publication of *Journeyman* for January, 1935, and I was making a selection for a third volume of short stories for publication in midyear; a volume of non-fiction, which could be classified as travel notes, seemed to be the most desirable type of book to write next.

At the end of six weeks of travel in the West, I went to Georgia to gather material for a pamphlet to be called *Tenant Farmer*. This tract was published the following May by The Phalanx Press.

When I arrived in New York late in October, Max Lieber met me with the news that a touring company of *Tobacco Road*, the play, had been closed in Chicago by order of Mayor Edward J. Kelly. The producers asked me to go to Chicago immediately to help with the defense of the play, and I took the Twentieth Century Limited on the New York Central the same day I arrived in New York. Jack Kirkland and Harry Oshrin thought that a way could be found to have the ban removed by legal action, but after considerable activity in the courts, the order was made permanent and the play did not reopen in Chicago during Mayor Kelly's lifetime.

I came back to New York at the end of a week to keep engagements to meet informally with English classes at New York University and Columbia University. While in New York I made the final selection of stories to be published in *Kneel to the Rising Sun*. There were seventeen short stories in the collection, one of which had been reprinted in *The Best Short Stories of 1934*, another in *The Best Short Stories of 1935*, and a third story was one which had appeared in *The O'Henry Memorial Award Prize Stories of 1934*. Most of these stories had previously appeared in, or were to be published in, *The American Mercury, The Anvil, Direction, Esquire, Literary America, New Masses, Red Book Magazine, Scribner's Magazine, Story, The Sunday Review*, and *Vanity Fair*. The book was brought out by Viking in June, 1935.

Journalism was still in my blood, probably a fomenting residue from my days on *The Atlanta Journal*, and I wanted to put it to use before writing the next novel. This urge to return temporarily to journalism was important to me; journalism had given me my first schooling in writing and it had never failed to renew my spirits. Max Lieber arranged for me to go South again in January and February, 1935, to write a series of feature articles for *The New York Post*. The publication of this series of articles in February about life on tenant farms in East Georgia was followed by a second and longer series written for *The New York Post* and published in April after several weeks of travel in Georgia, Alabama, and Mississippi.

When I arrived in New York for the publication of *Kneel to the Rising Sun*, Max Lieber told me that Viking had decided not to publish *Some American People*, the book of non-fiction. Max did not feel that it should be delayed, and he had already arranged for its publication by Robert M. McBride and Company. It was issued in October, 1935.

I had spent most of the summer in Mount Vernon and had made plans to go back to the West Coast for several months while deciding on the kind of book to write next. There had been few times in recent years when a number of ideas for books were not clamoring for attention, but I wanted to be sure now that the book I wrote next was of most importance to me. This time in California I did no motion-picture writing, and lived at a distance from Hollywood in San Fernando Valley from December, 1935, to April of the next year. Royalty from *Tobacco Road*, the play, was steadily increasing; after two years, the weekly amount was upward of a thousand dollars. Most of the money was invested, though none too wisely, in stocks and oil leases.

Call It Experience

By the beginning of April there was a clear idea in mind of the kind of book I wanted to undertake next and I went to New York and talked to Max Lieber about it. The book in mind was to be a factual study of people in cotton states living under current economic stress. It was my intention to show that the fiction I was writing was authentically based on contemporary life in the South. Furthermore, I felt that such a book should be thoroughly documented with photographs taken on the scene.

Although I had taken photographs to illustrate the articles written for *The New York Post*, the photography was decidedly the work of an amateur and I had no illusions about my ability in that field. I was strongly in favor of having the best obtainable photographer take the photographs for the book.

After considering several persons, Max Lieber arranged a meeting with Margaret Bourke-White, a spirited young woman with an engaging personality who had published a highly regarded volume of industrial photographs. In addition, she was well known for a volume of photographs of Russian industrial and agricultural operations. Margaret agreed to take the pictures for the book. It was decided that we would travel by automobile through the Southern states for about six weeks or two months.

After spending several weeks in Maine, I went to Georgia in July, 1936, to meet Margaret for the trip through the South. The book we were to collaborate on was to be called *You Have Seen Their Faces*.

The first three weeks of the tour through the cotton states with Margaret Bourke-White passed without incident. We planned to travel about three thousand miles, first westward from Georgia through Alabama, Mississippi, and Louisiana to Arkansas, then eastward through Tennessee and the Carolinas to Virginia. I had taken my Ford sedan to Georgia and it was heavily loaded with photographic equipment, numerous pieces of baggage, and three persons.

The third person in the party was the editorial assistant I had engaged for the trip; it was Sally's job to make accurate shorthand notes of conversations for the book.

Before leaving Augusta, Margaret and Sally apparently had come to a friendly understanding in regard to which one of them would ride in the rear seat and which one in the front seat. Sally had consented to ride in the rear all the time, saying in a joking manner that she was the hired girl and that untemperamental hired girls expected to sit at second table. Everyone seemed to be on friendly terms when we left Augusta; too late I realized that I probably could have forestalled any unpleasantness by offering at the start to sit in the rear seat myself and let someone else drive the car.

By the time we got to Little Rock, Sally was letting it be known that it was difficult for her to make her notes and copy them legibly in the jolting back seat. I tried to remedy an awkward situation by suggesting that we stay in Little Rock for several days. I thought the tension would disappear as soon as Sally had an opportunity to go to the hairdresser's and see a few motion pictures.

Even if I had thought of a better remedy, it probably would have been a failure too; Sally's dissatisfaction was undoubtedly destined to reach an abrupt conclusion in Little Rock. The first day we were there, Sally stated emphatically that she would not continue the trip if she had to sit on the back seat all the time; Margaret said she would probably lose interest in the whole venture if she had to sit in the rear seat any of the time. I tried to make light of the dispute by saying I felt honored to have two attractive young women arguing about which of them would sit in front with me, but that for the sake of harmony I would ride in the rear seat the remainder of the time. I was given to understand that I was to keep out of the argument.

At two-thirty in the morning, the night clerk of the Albert Pike Hotel, where we were staying, phoned me that a noisy disturbance was taking place on the sixth floor and that something had to be done about it.

"The disturbance will have to stop at once," the clerk repeated firmly. "The other guests are complaining."

"I'm not making a disturbance," I told him. "I'm in bed asleep."

"But one of the young ladies is making a very noisy one," he said. "One of the young ladies in your party. It's your responsibility."

"I'll try to find out about it," I promised.

Call It Experience

"It's up to you now," he warned me. "If you don't stop the disturbance, I'll have to take other steps."

I phoned Sally's room, but there was no answer. I dressed and walked down the hall. By the time I had got there, I could see no one and hear no disturbance; the only sound anywhere in the hotel was an occasional snore in one of the guest rooms. I went down to the lobby.

"You made a mistake," I told the clerk a little angrily. "There's nobody making a noise on the sixth floor."

He handed me an envelope.

"That's a note the young lady left for you," he said with a grin.

"What young lady?"

"The dark-haired one who just checked out. She called a taxi and went to the railroad station. She said she was taking a train in twenty minutes."

I sat down in one of the lobby chairs and read the note. Sally said she was quitting her job and going back home. She said she could work with one temperamental writer, or with one temperamental photographer, but that nobody could compel her to put up with two temperamental artists in the same automobile in the summertime in Arkansas.

Part Three: The Latter Years

I.

The lakes were blue and serene, the nights were clear and frosty, and the birch forests were brown and red and gold with autumn foliage in Northern New England in September. After a summer of travel in the simmering heat of the South, the State of Maine was cool and restful. It seemed to me then as though the most important undertaking in the world was making cider in the big wooden press behind the barn. I closed my typewriter and put it in a closet away from sight.

After a month of cider-making in the mornings and tramping through the woods in the afternoons and canoeing at twilight on Parker Lake, I could no longer hold back the desire to sit down at the typewriter. To me, writing had become as habit-forming as tobacco; I could abstain from writing for short intervals but always returned to it with renewed craving in the end.

I wanted to wait no longer after that to begin writing *You Have Seen Their Faces*, and early in October I left Mount Vernon and went to New York to live in an apartment at Forty-second Street and the East River. The Viking Press wished to bring out the book as soon as possible and publication had been scheduled for the spring of 1937. I hoped to finish the manuscript, select the photographs with Margaret Bourke-White, and write the captions during the last three months of 1936. Margaret was out of town on assignments for *Life* part of the time, which delayed the final selection of photographs, and I found myself involved in activities which in no way contributed to the completion of the book.

In October the French edition of *God's Little Acre*, translated by Maurice E. Coindreau, professor of French at Princeton University, was published in Paris by Gallimard. The edition contained a preface by André Maurois.

This was the first of my books to be translanted into another language, although all that I had written thus far had been published in England either by The Cresset Press, Martin Secker, or by Secker and Warburg, and Maurice Coindreau insisted that the event should be celebrated under his supervision. He came to New York and arranged an elaborately planned dinner at a penthouse restaurant on Central Park South. During the dinner he presented me with a copy of his translation and said that Gallimard had asked him to translate three more books of mine as soon as possible. Before he returned to Princeton, he arranged with Max Lieber to translate *American Earth*, *Tobacco Road*, and *We Are the Living*. This was the beginning of long and pleasant associations with Maurice and with the publishing house of Gallimard.

Long before the end of November, interruptions became more frequent and it began to look as if *You Have*

Seen Their Faces would not be finished in time for spring publication. One of the interruptions was The New York Times Book Fair of 1936, which was a literary circus presented in Rockefeller Center during the first week in November with authors and critics as performers. Marshall Best had urged me to accept an invitation to take part in the fair and I found that this activity consumed a week of time. I had never had any desire to talk about my own work, or to discuss literary matters in general—much less sit and listen to others engage in it for hours at a time—and the book fair convinced me that I should never again willingly consent to take part in such literary pastimes. I could always be sure of being happy and contented watching a baseball or football game.

But something even more disturbing was yet to come, and *You Have Seen Their Faces* suffered further delay. Earlier in the year, Max Lieber had failed to prevent me from signing a contract which bound me to go on a lecture tour during the 1936–37 season. Speaking from a public lecture platform was the last thing in the world I had any yearning for, and I must not have been in control of my mental faculties when I foolishly agreed to go on public exhibition in various cities of the country.

As the time for the first engagement drew near, I lay awake night after night in dread of the ordeal. No matter how many times I tried to think how I had come to consent to do such a thing, I could never recall what had prompted me to let myself be talked into it. I was sure I had no propensity for exhibitionism. A few days before the date for the lecture I even thought seriously of going to South America in order to escape from what was certain to be an agonizing experience.

Fortunately, the first engagement was canceled with the mutual consent of myself and the group that had hired me for exhibition. That stroke of good luck gave me the opportunity, and the courage as well, to plead with Frances Gossel, a lecture bureau manager, to release me from all the remaining engagements she had arranged. Wisely she released me from the contract; otherwise, everyone concerned undoubtedly would have had a trying time of it.

The first lecture had been scheduled to take place at Hamilton College, Clinton, New York. As it happened, Carl Sandburg was also beginning a lecture tour that season and I was asked if I would cancel my engagement at Hamilton in favor of Carl Sandburg.

My consent was instantaneous. I never asked anyone what the reason was for this last-minute request, but Leonard Lyons said in his syndicated newspaper column that it was because all I had to offer an audience was talk, while Carl Sandburg played a guitar with his lecture. Whatever the reason was, it enabled me to keep from having to suffer through an unpleasant ordeal that fall and winter.

2.

In spite of delays and interruptions, but mostly by grace of last-minute afflatus, *You Have Seen Their Faces* was ready early in 1937 for publication by The Viking Press.

Later in the year an inexpensive, paper-bound, news-stand edition was issued by Modern Age.

Eager by then to return to writing fiction, I began working on short stories in the spring. Monte Bour-jaily, who had been manager of a newspaper feature syndicate, and who was the founder and editor of *Mid-week Pictorial*, an illustrated weekly magazine devoted to fiction and topical articles, asked me to contribute to each issue of the new magazine for a year. Monte wanted me to write short stories rather than articles, but I found after writing half a dozen brief stories for the magazine that a weekly demand for fiction was too exacting. Regretfully I gave up writing both fiction and non-fiction for *Midweek Pictorial*. Working with Monte had been pleasant and profitable, but I did not feel that I wanted to devote my time exclusively to journalism.

Seventeen short stories had been written by the end of summer and Marshall Best told me that Viking wished to publish the collection the following year. The title I chose for the new book, which was the fourth volume of short stories to be published, was *Southways*. The stories in the collection first appeared in *The Atlantic Monthly, College Humor, Cosmopolitan, Direction, Esquire, Harper's Bazaar, Midweek Pictorial, The New Yorker, Parade, Red Book Magazine*, and *The Sunday Worker*. The placing of the stories in these magazines had been arranged by Max Lieber and the payment received for them ranged from ten dollars to fifteen hundred dollars.

Call It Experience

In September it became clearly evident that something had to be done immediately to bring order to the financial records I had attempted to keep during the past two years. My accounting consisted mostly of figures scrawled on checkbook stubs, there was no way to distinguish between professional and personal expenses, and I had no idea how much money had to be provided for income-tax payments. My current income amounted to approximately two thousand dollars weekly from royalties from *Tobacco Road*, the play, and about a thousand dollars monthly from book royalties, but only a portion of this had gone into savings. Besides, there were stacks of unanswered letters to be attended to. I had never employed a secretary, and I realized now that I would have to have help, or else have little time left for writing.

I moved that autumn to a larger apartment in the Mayflower, a residential hotel on Central Park West, and engaged an experienced secretary. Margaret Salter, a conscientious young woman who commuted from New Rochelle, spent the first several weeks sorting the accumulated mail and bringing order to my confused accounts.

After that, considerable time was devoted to writing replies to the more important letters. The remainder of the mail, as I found it, usually could be classified as follows: (a) letters asking outright for money; (b) letters offering the writer's life story for a fair consideration; and (c) anonymous letters accusing me of making money from the suffering of the human race in general or Southern tenant farmers in particular. The letters which did not fit into these categories were generally of an earnest nature, the writer asking only for an autograph, a theme paper suitable for an English class, or my signature on a petition of protest. The type of letter which gave me the most concern was the kind that demanded a stated sum of money to prevent bodily harm to a member of my family or to me.

Another legal document bearing my signature—possibly signed at the same time I wrote my name on Frances Gossel's lecture-tour contract—confronted me in the fall of 1937. This was an agreement authorizing Alfred Hayes and Leon Alexander to dramatize *Journeyman*. I had read the dramatization hurriedly and had approved it with certain reservations. The suggested changes had been made in the script and Sam Byrd, who had left his featured role in *Tobacco Road* after four years, had signed a contract with the dramatists to produce it.

I had no more desire to become involved with play production on Broadway then than I had had at the time the dramatization of *Tobacco Road* was being staged, but Sam Byrd waged such a persistent campaign by telephone, by mail, and in person that I finally agreed to help bring *Journeyman* to the theater. I thought Sam would be satisfied if I invested a few thousand dollars in the production, but he said this was not sufficient. He insisted, in addition to an investment, that I help revise the script of the play, pass on the casting, and attend readings and rehearsals. All of this was a full day's stint, for two months, from midmorning to midnight.

Journeyman, the play, opened at the Fulton Theatre,

in New York, on the wintry evening of January 30, 1938. During the dress rehearsal the previous night, the dramatists and the director had loudly renounced any connection with the play, at the same time denouncing the personalities of anyone within hearing distance, all in terms barely short of physical violence. Sam had dismissed the turbulent brawl as being merely a temperamental flare-up common on Broadway on the eve of an opening, and he remained cool and confident and as enthusiastic as ever. The reviews of the opening performance were almost wholly unfavorable; in fact, so strongly worded were they to that effect that there seemed little purpose in opening the doors of the Fulton for a second-night performance.

Sam was a determined man, however, and he would not permit himself to be discouraged by critical panning. He said there were many plays in the history of the theater that had survived unfavorable notices and lived to flourish for many months, and that he wanted to see *Journeyman* take its place among that select group. It was Sam's plan to raise additional money for salaries and theater rent so the play could be kept going for a full week, his reasoning being that the damaging reviews would be forgotten at the end of that time and the box office would show improvement. Sam asked me to get five thousand dollars quickly somewhere, somehow.

Ordinarily it was not an easy task to persuade anyone to back a play even before it opened; it was next to impossible to find anyone to provide several thousand dollars to keep a play going once it had opened to definitely adverse notices.

"Sam," I said, "I don't know where to find anybody who would put money into a play that's already a cold turkey."

"It's easy," he assured me. "You can find backers on Broadway for a hundred-thousand-dollar production of a dog scratching fleas—and he wouldn't have to be a big shaggy dog, either. It's merely a matter of getting to the right people and talking fast. That's all there is to financing on Broadway."

"You've been on Broadway a lot longer than I have," I told him. "Maybe you ought to be the one to get to the right people and do the talking."

"I've got to stick close to the theater and keep my eyes on the box office," he said. "It's just as important for a producer to watch that box office as it is for a sea captain to watch the barometer."

As I had feared, I provided much of the money from my own savings. At the end of the first week, seventy-five hundred dollars was the amount needed to keep *Journeyman* going for the second week. Soon after that my savings had vanished and other sources dried up and the play closed at the end of the third week. As I watched the scenery being hauled away, I vowed to be more careful of my investments in the future. And especially to shun the privilege of backing a play on Broadway.

3.

Having been confined to New York for more than a year, I was restless with the urge to travel again. The manuscript of *Southways* had been delivered to Viking for publication in June, 1938, and I did not like the prospect of settling down to the six- or eight-month task of writing a novel until first I had taken another trip somewhere.

I was thirty-four years old and had never been outside the United States and Canada; under the circumstances it was not difficult to convince myself that the time to go abroad was at hand. I suggested to Margaret Bourke-White that we collaborate on a second book of photographs-and-text. We both felt that *You Have Seen Their Faces* had proved to be a successful collaboration and that it should be followed by a second volume similar in plan and different in subject. After considering several possibilities, we decided to go to Czechoslovakia and spend about two months gathering material for a travel book.

We sailed on the S.S. *Normandie* of the French Line late in May and went by train through France and Germany to Czechoslovakia. It was June when we arrived in Prague, but it was cold and damp at that time of year in Middle Europe and snow still lay on the northern slopes of the undulating hills and high mountains. The wooded countryside, green with pines and white with splotches of snow, looked much like Northern New England before an April thaw.

Speaking no language other than English, I soon found that I was not going to acquire any facility with the Czech or the Slovak language in a few weeks' time. Both languages were Slavic, and even my limited knowledge of Latin and French was of little aid. However, there were many persons in Prague who spoke English well. Whenever I needed any help, I called on Jiri Pober, a literary agent, or on Franz Weiskopf, the editor of a daily newspaper. The Czech translation of *God's Little Acre* had been published in Prague in 1937 by Lidova Kultura and Jiri Pober's agency had arranged for its publication.

Once we began traveling in the central and eastern regions of Czechoslovakia, the language barrier at times became a serious matter. In Bohemia and Moravia there was little difficulty in making ourselves understood by taxi drivers, policemen, and restaurant waiters, but in the two eastern provinces, Slovakia and Carpathian Ruthenia, inhabitants who had any appreciable acquaintance with the English language were not easy to find. Even hotel porters, who in Europe take pride in their ability to attend to the ordinary needs of foreigners, often shrugged their shoulders and gave up.

Obtaining a meal in a hotel or cafe, especially in Carpathian Ruthenia, was at times a nerve-racking and time-consuming ordeal. Fortunately, it happened that I did like schnitzel, which could be found almost without exception on every menu in the provinces, and this was about the only food the waiter and I had any mutual understanding of. Waiters themselves, for some reason, had a fondness for schnitzel and held it in high esteem regardless of whether they themselves or the customers were eating it. They always seemed pleased when I ordered it, and I noticed that schnitzel-eating diners seemed to receive as a matter of course more than ordinary attention and respect.

For nearly a month I contented myself with Vienna schnitzel for lunch and dinner, as well as for a midnight snack occasionally, and most of the time the only way I succeeded in getting an egg in the morning for breakfast was to order Holstein schnitzel. This dish ordinarily, in that region of Middle Europe, was served with one or two fried eggs on the schnitzel; at other times it was served with poached eggs on top.

Early one morning in Uzhgorod, near the Russian Ukraine, I attempted to get eggs without schnitzel in the hotel restaurant. As much as I liked schnitzel prepared in any style, eating it two times a day had become sufficient.

"Oeuf mit out schnitzel," I told the waiter, enunciating clearly and distinctly. "Much oeuf mit out."

"Nein schnitzel?" he said, shaking his head a little.

I thought of trying to expand my pidgin language for the occasion, but I was afraid of confusing the waiter.

"Much oeuf mit out," I repeated.

"Khorosho," he muttered without enthusiasm.

"Nein schnitzel—much oeuf," I reminded him firmly.

"Tak," he said as we walked away.

Call It Experience

Twenty minutes later, smiling broadly, he returned and placed a soup dish before me. The dish was filled to the brim with red caviar.

"Nein schnitzel," the waiter said, bowing solemnly.

"Tak," I said, looking at the beady, uncooked food.

I put a small portion of the caviar in my mouth and began chewing it experimentally.

"You like?" the waiter asked, speaking English for the first time.

"If you understand English that well, why did you bring me fish eggs instead of chicken eggs?"

He shrugged his shoulders as if he did not understand a word of what I had said. While he stood nearby grinning happily, I ate the great quantity of red fish eggs with a spoon.

After traveling on most of the principal railway lines and many of the branch lines in Czechoslovakia, eating schnitzel at dozens of depot cafes and hotel restaurants, we went to Budapest and took the Orient Express to Paris. I spent a good part of the time in Paris at Safe de La Paix eating ham and eggs. Late in August we returned to the United States on the S.S. *Aquitania* of the Cunard Line.

I was anxious to begin writing the book on Czechoslovakia without delay and at the same time I wanted to avoid interruptions. With that purpose in mind I rented a cottage on Pratt's Island, which was near Noroton and off the Connecticut shore of Long Island Sound.

At the end of two months the first draft of the book was written, and then, since winter was closing in on the wind-swept island, I bought a white Cape Cod house on a wooded hilltop in Darien for twenty thousand dollars. By the end of the year, the text was finished and the photographs selected. The title that Margaret and I chose for the book was *North of the Danube*. It was published by The Viking Press in April, 1939, after the occupation of Czechoslovakia by Germany.

4.

As it sometimes happens, no matter how friendly are the personal and professional relations existing between publisher and author, contracts expire and are not renewed. This is not an unusual occurrence when the enthusiasm of one of the principals wanes. And in such cases dissatisfaction with the performance of the other principal is more than apt to follow swiftly. Ordinarily this has to do with the failure of an author's books to be bought by the public in desired quantities; it is then customary for the author to blame the publisher or for the publisher to blame the author. When they put the blame on each other, the end of the association is not far off.

The Viking Press was rightly displeased because I had not written a novel since *Journeyman*, which had been published in 1935 and reissued in 1938, and no doubt as equally displeased because I was devoting most of my time to writing non-fiction books such as *North*

Call It Experience
of the Danube and *You Have Seen Their Faces.* Max
Lieber was unhappy because Harold Guinzburg and
Marshall Best were not inclined to accept his proposals
for the terms of a new contract. I was not happy because
I believed that Viking did not show sufficient interest
in the books I wrote. It was inevitable under these circumstances that enthusiasm on the part of both Viking and
myself gradually diminished and finally vanished completely.

I did not have the same feeling about withdrawing
from Viking as I had had at the time I ended my association with Max Perkins and Charles Scribner's Sons. I
had come to look upon publishing as being more properly a professional or business phase of writing than it
was a personal one.

It was spring then and dogwood was in blossom in
Connecticut. *North of the Danube* had been published
and I had begun writing a novel in Darien. The novel
was to be called *Trouble in July* and it represented another phase of life in the cycloramic depiction of the
South begun with *Tobacco Road* and continued with
God's Little Acre and *Journeyman.* The story told in
Trouble in July was one of small-town politics and its
effect on the lives and character of the people in the
community.

In the warm days of spring in Connecticut I wrote out
of doors in the sun on a moss-covered boulder overlooking
Long Island Sound, completing the first draft of the
book in about two months' time. Before starting the

second and final draft, I decided it would be wise to come to some decision regarding a new publishing contract either with Viking or with another house.

Max Lieber and I had several meetings with Harold and Marshall. During the course of one of these, Max asked Harold if he intended to publish *Trouble in July*.

"I suppose we will publish this new Caldwell item," Harold told him.

"Item?" Max said, sitting up erectly. "You call a novel like *Trouble in July* an item? Skinny and I didn't come here to peddle merchandise. We're here to talk about a novel, Harold."

As usual when such occasions arose, Marshall soothed tempers with a humorous remark that brought forth chuckles from all sides of the room.

However, Max remained firm in his insistence that we be paid a larger sum of advance royalty for each new book written and that we receive increased royalty percentage. I added to the atmosphere of dissatisfaction by saying I wished to establish and edit a series of regional books that would have the general title of *American Folkways*.

This series was a project which had interested me ever since I began traveling in the United States and had observed the remarkable differences in regional life. I wanted to plan a series of studies, to be written by authors well acquainted with the localities in which they lived, and which would describe and interpret the indigenous quality of life in America. Shortly before his death in 1938, Thomas Wolfe had said he wished to contribute the first volume to the series; because of Tom's death, I had delayed the attempt to launch *American Folkways*.

The purpose of these books, aside from being interesting and readable, was to describe the cultural influences implanted by the original settlers and their descendants and to explain the manner in which life in one region of the country differed from the way of life in another region. The sum of these studies, it seemed to me, would reveal the ingrained character of America. I believed this program could be accomplished in twenty-five or thirty volumes. Harold and Marshall were not eager to undertake such a large and costly publishing venture under my editorship, and so in the end they came to look with disfavor upon each and all of the proposals presented by Max Lieber and myself. Consequently, still friendly, we agreed to let the original contract expire and not to enter into a new one.

I stayed in Darien during the summer of 1939 and finished *Trouble in July* before Labor Day. Not only was it the first novel I had written since 1935; more than that, it was the first book I had written since 1930 for which I had no publisher. Random House had offered to submit a contract for my approval, but I hesitated to enter into an agreement with any publisher until I was sure in my own mind that I would be satisfied with the association over a long period of time. It was my hope to maintain a friendly connection indefinitely, not merely for three years or for three books as I had in the past, with my next publisher.

Random House was the publisher of the Modern Library, a collection of well-made and inexpensive reprints, and I had known Bennett Cerf and Donald Klopfer, the editors, since *God's Little Acre* was issued in a Modern Library edition in 1934. I was on the verge of entering into an agreement with Bennett and Donald, they having offered terms better than I had ever received from any other publisher, and I probably would have signed a contract with Random House if I had not happened to meet Charles H. Duell at a dinner where we both were guests of Emily Clark.

Charlie Duell told me of the plans that he, together with Samuel Sloan and Charles A. Pearce, had made to found a new publishing house. I had known Cap Pearce for many years and had much respect for his abilities and his foresightedness as an editor. I told Charlie that I was looking for a new publisher and that perhaps a young and aggressive publishing house was looking for me. He said at once that I could write my own contract with Duell, Sloan and Pearce. We shook hands to bind our understanding and I told him that I would ask Max Lieber to draw up a contract with him immediately. The agreement, containing all the features that Max and I desired at the time, including the program to launch *American Folkways* and to issue from two to four volumes of the series yearly, was signed a few days later.

The first book to be given to Duell, Sloan and Pearce was *Trouble in July* and it was scheduled for publication on February 23, 1940. In order to get *American Folkways* established as soon as possible, I left Darien late in October, 1939, on a cross-country automobile trip in

search of a number of able writers to contribute volumes
to the series.

5.

Five weeks after leaving Connecticut, five authors had
consented to write the first five volumes of *American
Folkways*. Jean Thomas, of Kentucky, was writing *Blue
Ridge Country* and Otto Ernest Rayburn, of Arkansas,
was writing *Ozark Country*. I had spent several days at
the University of Oklahoma, in Norman, talking to Stanley Vestal, who had agreed to write *Short Grass Country*, and a week in Santa Fe, New Mexico, the home of
Haniel Long, who was writing *Piñon Country*. In Los
Angeles, Edwin Corle had contracted to write *Desert
Country*.

Edwin Corle was the only one of these five authors I
had not corresponded with or had not known previously.
Ed was somewhat belligerent when I finished explaining why I had come to see him.

"I'd like to write the book," he said, "but nobody's
going to edit my work. If there's ever editing to be done,
I do it myself."

"I'm not doing the kind of editing you're talking about,
Ed," I assured him. "I think every *American Folkways*
author should plan his own book. All I do is offer suggestions if I'm asked for them."

"Well, that's different," he said. "I've wanted to write

Call It Experience

a book about the desert country of the Southwest for ten years—and now I'm going to do it for *American Folkways* even if you and I get into a quarrel over every chapter I write."

It was the last of November then and I was confident that the books being written would give *American Folkways* a successful start. These five books were published by Duell, Sloan and Pearce during 1941 and 1942. In the course of the next ten years, a total of twenty-five volumes was published in the series.

When I left California, I stopped in Arizona during the first week in December to visit Harry Behn. Harry had bought a home in Tucson and it was the first time I had seen him since he left Hollywood. He had initiated radio writing courses and radio discussion programs at the University of Arizona and he was the head of that department.

During the week I spent in Tucson, Harry tried unsuccessfully to persuade me to buy a home on the desert and live there part of each year. It was my first visit to the Southern Arizona desert and I was not impressed by the famed grandeur of its barren expanse and towering dry mountains. After thirty-seven years in the South and East, I sould not understand why anyone would willingly leave a country of leafy trees and green grass for the sun-baked sand and prickly cactus of a desert. However, when I left Tucson, I had the uneasy premonition that I was going to miss being able to watch the shadows come to the purple mountains in late afternoon. After all, there was an inescapable fascination

186

about the constantly deepening purple that merged into clear star-lit nights.

After a week in Arizona, I started driving to Florida. I planned to go to Miami Beach and to stay there for about two weeks before going back to Connecticut in January. The distance from Tucson to El Paso, Texas, was more than three hundred miles. Several hours before reaching El Paso, I began to feel dizzy and weak, and a number of times I stopped the car beside the highway until I felt capable of driving again. Seizures of intense feverishness and dizziness came at half-hour intervals. I did not think I was going to die, but I had never before felt so close to it.

I had intended stopping at a hotel in El Paso, but when I got out of my car at the Plaza in the center of the city and tried to stand up, my knees buckled under me. I knew then that something was seriously wrong. After sitting in the car for a quarter of an hour, I asked a taxi driver where the nearest hospital was located.

"Three blocks from here, on the right-hand side of the street," he said, pointing across the Plaza. "You couldn't miss it if you tried."

My sight was blurred and I could see nothing beyond the Plaza.

"What's the name of the hospital?" I asked him.

"Hotel Dieu."

I could sense a feverish clouding of my mind as I shook my head at the taxi driver.

"But I don't want to go to a hotel—I want a hospital. Where's the nearest one?"

"That's what I'm telling you, bub," he said earnestly. "Hotel Dieu—up that street three blocks. You can't miss it, I tell you."

"You keep on saying it's a hotel," I protested weakly. "Where's the hospital?"

Exasperated, he took a deep breath and expelled it noisily.

"Bub," he said slowly, "don't you know what you hear when you hear it? I said that's a hospital. Hotel Dieu. It's the name of the hospital. Get it now?"

I gazed blankly at the taxi driver, vaguely wondering why any man would torment another human being as he was doing.

"What's the name of another hospital?" I begged.

"The City-County Hospital," he said, shaking his head to himself. "Maybe you like that name better. It's all the same to me if you do, bub. Take this other street for about three miles and you can't miss it."

I drove away in the direction of the City-County Hospital and found it shortly after midnight. I left my car in a parking lot in front of the building and staggered into the receiving room.

There were two nurses and an intern on duty. All of them seemed to be suspicious of me as they watched me walk unsteadily into the brightly lighted room. The intern first smelled my breath, and then he led me into an adjoining room and took my temperature. He said it was dangerously above normal and that I would have to stay under observation until morning. I was so glad to be where I was that I did not care then what the diagnosis was going to reveal.

A nurse and one of the staff physicians woke me up at dawn. The tall angular doctor, who was about my own age, laughed at me for a long time before telling me that I had chicken pox. Later that morning he came back and tacked an Infants' Ward sign on the door of my room and informed me that I would be required to stay in the hospital for about a week.

When I paid my account and got ready to leave at the end of a week, a nurse told me that my physician had contracted chicken pox from me and had been put in quarantine. I drove to a drugstore and bought a rubber teething ring and had it sent to the doctor in care of the Infants' Ward.

I reached Florida shortly before Christmas Day and stayed at the Wofford Hotel on Miami Beach. I had been there for several days when a raven-haired girl of twenty came to the hotel and asked for an interview for a student publication at the University of Miami. Her name was Mildred Zinn. She talked so interestingly and intelligently during the hour-long interview that, when she was leaving, I told her there was a job for her as an editorial assistant any time she wanted to come to work for me. She said she expected to graduate from the University of Miami at mid-term in February and after that she would be looking for a job. Mildred came to Darien at the end of February.

Call It Experience

6.

There were few times during the twelve-month period beginning in the spring of 1940 and ending in the spring of 1941 when I was not traveling or writing. After the publication of *Trouble in July* in February, 1940, Mildred Zinn and I began the three-month task of selecting, from magazines and from four previously published volumes, the work which I wished to include in a collection containing seventy-five short stories. Cap Pearce and I had already decided to call the book *Jackpot*, and Duell, Sloan and Pearce planned to publish the seven-hundred-and-fifty-six-page collection in the early fall. In addition, Sam Sloan had persuaded me to promise to write a brief preface to each of the seventy-five stories.

There were one hundred short stories from which the selection was to be made, that being the number of published stories which I had set in 1930 as a goal for accomplishment, and I wished to choose the best seventy-five of these for *Jackpot*. It soon became evident that the selection of the stories and the writing of the prefaces was no ordinary task. Mildred had found, to begin with, that several of the stories originally published in magazines had not been reprinted in book form and it was not always easy for her to find copies of some of them. The stories which she could not obtain otherwise were copied at the New York Public Library.

In addition to her work on *Jackpot*, Mildred was at

the same time helping me plan and select possible writers for the next several volumes of *American Folkways*. The three books that were planned at this time for the series were *High Border Country*, by Eric Thane, *Palmetto Country*, by Stetson Kennedy, and *Mormon Country*, by Wallace Stegner.

In June I left Darien for a vacation in Mexico; I had looked forward to the trip as being a vacation from writing but I soon found that I was working on short stories most of the time. I traveled in the states of San Luis Potosi, Coahuila, Chihuahua, Durango, and Zacatecas for several weeks and then went back to New York to find that Sam Sloan had arranged for me to take part in a number of radio programs.

Of the several radio programs I took part in, I found *Information Please* and *Town Meeting of the Air* to be the most interesting. After these appearances, I found that I did not dislike radio, and had none of the objections to it that had led me to avoid lecture tours, but nevertheless radio still did not appeal to me as strongly as writing did. When I asked Sam Sloan why he had urged me to appear on radio programs, he explained that it was desirable, from a publisher's point of view, for an author to take part in such activities since radio and newspaper interviews had proved to be an important part of a publisher's promotion program.

I had written five or six short stories in Mexico, which afterward were published in *Harper's Magazine* and *Town and Country* and *Esquire*, but nevertheless I was anxious to begin writing another book. In September I

suggested to Margaret Bourke-White that we collaborate on a third volume of photographs-and-text. We decided this time to remain in the United States and to
travel by railway and airplane for three months.

The trip began in Cedar Rapids, Iowa, in October, and
ended in Columbia, South Carolina, in December. During those three months we traveled in Kansas, Colorado,
Utah, Nevada, Arizona, New Mexico, Texas, Arkansas,
Mississippi, Florida, Georgia, and the Carolinas. The
book, which was to be called *Say! Is This the U.S.A.?*,
was written in the months of January and February,
1941, and it was scheduled for publication by Duell,
Sloan and Pearce in June of that year.

While we were completing *Say! Is This the U.S.A.?*,
Margaret said she would like to collaborate on a fourth
book of photographs-and-text and this time to go to Russia for the material. She had traveled in the Soviet Union,
but I had not, and the prospect of taking such a trip appealed to me. We went to Washington and made appli-
cation for visas at the embassy of the U.S.S.R.

Constantin Oumansky, the Soviet ambassador at the
time, showed no enthusiasm for our plans to go to Russia to gather material for a book. First he said that such
a trip at that particular time was not one that I should
want my wife to take because of the difficulties of travel;
I reminded him that Margaret had done considerable
traveling about the world both before we were married
in 1939 and since then, and that she was probably a more
experienced traveler than I. Next he tried to discourage
us by saying he could promise to get us into Russia but

could not promise to get us out. Finally he warned us that we might find ourselves being prisoners of war in the Soviet Union, but said that if we actually succeeded in getting to China, the visas would be given to us by the Soviet ambassador in Chungking.

We began making preparations for the trip immediately. The manuscript of *Say! Is This the U.S.A.?* was given to Cap Pearce and I went to see a performance of *Tobacco Road* on Broadway for the last time. The play, which had already established a record at the time for the number of performances given, was to close in May after a run of seven and a half years on Broadway. In spite of the fact that the stage scenery looked more shabby and tattered than ever, and even though many members of the cast had played their parts for such a long time that they gave the impression of being bored with their jobs, the play still appealed to me as strongly as it had the first time I saw it presented.

In mid-March, Margaret and I went by United Airlines to Los Angeles to board the S.S. *Lurline* for Honolulu. From Hawaii we had passage on the China Clipper of Pan American Airways to the Orient.

The Chinese-Japanese War was in progress in 1941 and it was difficult to get passage by airplane, the only means of travel across China, from Hong Kong to Chungking. We waited a week in Hong Kong before we finally got space on a cargo plane carrying bales of Chinese Nationalist currency to the wartime capital at Chungking. In Chungking, where we spent most of the time in crowded caves during Japanese bombing raids, the Soviet ambassador stamped U.S.S.R. visas in our passports after a wait of eight days.

We then started to Alma-Ata, the capital of the Soviet Republic of Kazakh, in a small one-engine plane of the Chinese-operated Eurasia Aviation Corporation Airline. The ancient German-made aircraft had engine trouble at Lanchow, Province of Kansu, China, and there we waited nine days for another plane of similar type to take us to Hami, Province of Sinkiang, which was the interchange point with a Russian airline.

Over the Gobi Desert in Mongolia a sandstorm forced the Chinese pilot to make an unscheduled landing at a Mongolian military airfield. The door of the plane was promptly sealed by soldiers when we landed, and we sat there wondering if Constantin Oumansky had Mongolia in mind when he said we might find ourselves being held prisoners of war.

After three and a half hours in the airtight plane we were taken in a truck to an army compound and kept under guard until the sandstorm passed away the next day. The twenty-four-hour delay caused us to miss the connection in Hami, and we had to wait there six days for the next weekly plane to Alma-Ata.

Alice-Leone Moats, who had been seeking a visa at the Soviet embassy when we left Chungking, had caught up with us in Lanchow, and in Hami we passed the time by playing Chinese checkers and eating Russian caviar. A pint of tasty black caviar could be bought in Hami for the Sinkiang equivalent of one American dollar.

The three of us were delayed once more in Alma-Ata

while our baggage and visas were inspected, but on the
fourth day our passports and baggage were returned to
us and space was provided on the plane to Moscow. The
plane was a new two-engine Russian-made Douglas
DC-3. The only noticeable difference between it and its
American counterpart was that the Russian plane did
not provide seat belts for passengers.

After two days of flight and an overnight stop at
Aktyubinsk, we arrived in Moscow the first week of
May, 1941.

7.

The openhanded rewards in the Soviet Union for being
a published writer were overwhelming. Communist
writers, in a communist state, might have expected favored treatment, but I was not a communist, and so I was
unprepared for such a windfall. Margaret Bourke-White
and I had gone there for the workaday purpose of photographing and writing a book, not for the diversion of
living in luxury in Moscow, and then suddenly the means
for luxurious living were thrust upon me. It seemed
foolish after that to ask the waiter not to bring caviar and
champagne for a midnight snack.

I asked Eugene Petrov, an English-speaking Russian
novelist and journalist, why writers in the Soviet Union
seemingly received a greater amount of royalties than
the average American author. He said the reason was
that when a Soviet author's book was published, that fact

indicated that the book was acceptable state propaganda, and consequently it was issued in editions of hundreds of thousands of copies.

"But my books are American," I said. "Why should they be published here at all?"

"American novels in Russia are pro-Soviet today, anti-Soviet tomorrow. It all depends on politics."

After being in Moscow for only a few days, I was informed by Mikhail Apletin, the secretary of the foreign section of the Union of Soviet Writers, that I had a large ruble account as the result of accumulated royalties. It was the practice in the Soviet Union to publish books by foreign authors without the formality of negotiations or contracts, but royalty was strictly accounted for and deposited in the state bank to the authors' credit. In order to obtain this royalty, it was necessary to go to Russia and apply for it in person.

Mikhail Apletin gave me a list of my Russian-translated publications. *American Earth* had been published in Moscow in 1936 in an illustrated edition, and reissued in 1937 in a trade edition; *Tobacco Road* had been published in a large edition in 1938; *Trouble in July* had been published in 1940; pamphlet editions of short stories, selections from *We Are the Living* and *Kneel to the Rising Sun*, had been issued in 1938 and 1941; and a number of monthly magazines and weekly newspapers had published short stories.

When I was asked at Goslitizdat, the state fiction publishing house, how many rubles I wished to draw, I said I would take all in my account. I had given no thought to how much this would amount to, but I should have guessed it would be the equivalent of a few hundred dollars at the most, and sufficient to pay part of my living and traveling expenses while I was in the country.

To start with, what might have been, at other times and in other places, the simple procedure of drawing earned royalty in the offices of the publishing house developed into a lavish, Asiatic-flavored ceremony that began at one-thirty in the afternoon and ended six hours later.

Samples of various types of dry and sweet vodka were served at the large conference table and, once that started, no one seemed eager to put an end to it. After nearly an hour of toasting Jack London, Shakespeare, Upton Sinclair, Mikhail Sholokhov, Confucius, and numerous others mutually acceptable as subjects for admiration, the type of vodka most favored by the dozen editors, assistant editors, and interpreters present was concentrated on for another hour. By that time iced black caviar was being served in large crystal bowls; and soon waiters were bringing in pink and white champagne. As soon as one caviar bowl was partly empty, the waiters brought in another heaping one. The supply of iced champagne seemed likewise to be unlimited. Toward evening, chocolate candy and syrupy Georgian coffee were served.

Finally, in the early evening, a cashier and his assistant entered the conference room carrying bundled rubles. The currency was tied in neat bundles of ten-ruble notes, and each stack contained a thousand rubles. After the rubles had been carefully arranged in rows on the green felt-covered table, I was asked to sign a receipt for the money.

I was given a suitcase in which to carry the money home in a taxi and advised to keep it in the safe at the National Hotel since I would have a trying time as a foreigner if I attempted to deposit it in a bank. Once drawn, the money could not be returned to the state publishing house without much difficulty, and it could not be taken from the country. I gave about half of the money to the hotel manager for safekeeping and distributed the remaining bundles under a white bear rug, in closets, and behind the pictures on the wall. It was not long until I discovered that the cost of goods and services, paid for with blocked rubles, was higher than I had expected. By the time I left Russia, I was not only exchanging dollars for rubles at an unfavorable rate, but spending more for professional expenses than I was earning in both the Soviet Union and the United States.

Margaret and I had planned to travel through Great Russia, White Russia, the Ukraine, the Caucasus, and parts of Siberia, but in the end, after waiting three weeks, we were glad to get travel permits to take a trip of two thousand miles to Kharkov, Tbilisi, and the Black Sea. Foreign newspaper correspondents who had been in Moscow for many months, and who had not succeeded in buying a train ticket to Leningrad, told us that we were fortunate to get permission to go beyond the Moscow suburbs.

After having waited three weeks, I went to the government press office and asked when Margaret and I could expect to receive permission to begin our trip.

A solemn-faced young man of about twenty-seven, who spoke English clearly and precisely, said right away that Alice-Leone Moats had not applied for a permit to travel to Kharkov, Tbilisi, and the Black Sea with us, and, for that reason, we could not leave Moscow until she did so. I told him that I knew of no reason why Alice-Leone should apply for a permit to travel with us.

The young man looked at me gravely. "But you are personally responsible for the conduct of Miss Moats. It would clearly be impossible for you to fulfill your obligation if she were in Moscow and you were in a distant region of the Soviet Union."

"Why am I responsible for Alice-Leone Moats?"

"Because you are her employer."

"I am not," I said. "She's self-employed. She came here to do her own writing."

Frowning at me, the young man shook his head. "You are wrong," he said. "You have made an inaccurate statement."

"I don't know why you say that," I protested. "I never saw Alice-Leone Moats before in my life until I met her in China. It was merely a coincidence that we came to Russia on the same airplane."

"Mr. Caldwell, it is useless for you to persist in denying facts," he said solemnly. "The true facts of the matter are clear. She will have to apply for a travel permit and go wherever you go in the Soviet Union."

"I don't think Alice-Leone would be interested in that."

"She can't stay in Moscow if you leave. And you can't leave unless she goes with you."

"Something's wrong," I told him. "Something's badly mixed up."

"It's clear that you brought her to the Soviet Union with you. That much we know. And under our regulations, you are personally responsible for her political conduct while she's within our borders."

"I did not bring her," I said flatly.

The young man opened a file and took out a number of official-looking papers and spread them on the table between us.

"Here before us is the absolute proof," he said, watching me gravely. "You can't deny the truth of the official report."

"Tell me what it says in the report."

"It states here as a matter of official record that Alice-Leone Moats was granted permission to enter the Soviet Union at Alma-Ata at your request. The reason stated here for your request is that she is your secretary."

"Somebody's pulled somebody's leg at Alma-Ata," I told him. "I never made such a request. And she's not my secretary, either."

"The official record cannot be wrong. That's impossible. It states here very clearly the true facts of the case."

"Somebody else stated them then," I told him. "I know I didn't."

"Miss Moats would not have been permitted to enter

the Soviet Union if you or somebody else had not made the request."

"Then you'd better ask somebody else about it," I said. "It's something somebody else may know a lot more about than I do."

"This is a very serious matter," he said, shaking his head. "If you disclaim any responsibility for the political conduct of Alice-Leone Moats, it means she is vouched for by no one. She'll have to leave the Soviet Union at once."

"If you're going to be the one to tell her, you'd better be prepared to duck fast when she starts throwing furniture around. I don't think she'll like the suggestion. Besides, if she was clever enough to get into the country, she's probably clever enough to find a way to stay. You know how these American girls are when they want something."

The young man gathered the papers together and stood up. He still did not smile.

"Your travel permits will be ready tomorrow," he stated. "They will permit you and Margaret Bourke-White to carry out the plan you have filed. There will be no permit for Alice-Leone Moats to travel to Kharkov, Tbilisi, and the Black Sea. Other plans will be made for Miss Moats."

8.

The outbreak of the Russian-German War on June 22, 1941, brought to an abrupt end the plans Margaret Bourke-White and I had made for gathering material for a book during the remainder of the summer. When the war started, we were at Sukhumi, a resort on the Georgian shore of the Black Sea, and we got ready to leave on the first available train. We were able to secure berths in a sleeping car, but food was difficult to obtain. It seemed to me that I spent most of the waking hours dashing to the hot-water spigot and standing in line for boiled water to make tea each time the train stopped at a station. Food was obtained by leaning out the sleeping-car window and begging a grandmotherly-looking woman to sell me two dippers of kasha instead of only one. The trip northward through the Ukraine lasted four days and nights and we arrived in Moscow on the morning of June 28.

When I got to the National Hotel, there were a number of radiograms from the United States. Most of these messages were from newspaper syndicates and editors offering me a job as correspondent. There was only a handful of American newspapermen in the Soviet Union and there were many more jobs available than there were reporters to fill them. I went to see the United States ambassador to the Soviet Union, Lawrence A. Steinhardt, and he had additional radiograms for Margaret and me.

Margaret started at once on photographic assignments for *Life*.

After considering the offers I had received, I undertook to file daily radiogram reports for North American Newspaper Alliance, a syndicate; to broadcast twice daily to New York via short wave for Columbia Broadcasting System; and, finally, to write articles for *Life*. With so much to do day and night, I used a portion of my royalties to buy a secondhand automobile and engaged a chauffeur and a secretary. I noticed in the beginning that my chauffeur carried a pistol in a holster under his chauffeur's jacket, but it was several weeks before I found out that he was a corporal in the Red Army and had been assigned to me as a bodyguard. My secretary, English-speaking and highly intelligent, had been assigned by the press office to do the work I required. The large corner suite at the National Hotel, which had an iron balcony overlooking Red Square and the Kremlin, was soon in such disorder that it looked more like an untended newspaper office than a Louis Quinze bedroom-and-parlor.

Of the three assignments I had undertaken, broadcasting for CBS was the most difficult, time-consuming, and hazardous of all. The scripts of the broadcasts had to be submitted, in triplicate, to the censors at the government press office an hour before broadcast time, and, as it frequently happened, when words or sentences or complete scripts were censored, I had to fill in sufficient wordage for a full broadcast and resubmit the script for censorship.

Call It Experience

The scheduled broadcast times were at three o'clock in the afternoon and at three in the morning. The job became even more difficult at night when German air raids on Moscow began early in July. The radio transmitting station we were using was bombed at exactly three o'clock in the morning two weeks after the raiding began and we had to move to another transmitting station. The latter was a well-known Moscow landmark, and, understandably, one of the prime targets of the raiders. Going to and returning from the radio station became a harrowing night-time experience during the next three months. Spent anti-aircraft fragments falling in the blacked-out streets were far more numerous than German bombs. The eerie whizzing sound of steel cables that had been shot loose from captive barrage balloons was not comforting.

I had been filing daily wireless reports to North American Newspaper Alliance for several days when I began receiving long radiograms from Ralph Ingersoll, the editor of *PM* in New York. At first these messages were casual and friendly and merely informed me that *PM* was in need of a Moscow correspondent. The next messages asked me to help find somebody at once for the job.

A few days later Ralph's radiograms became more urgent and very strongly worded, and they no longer conveyed friendly good wishes for my health and safety. Ralph said bluntly that he wanted me to resign from my NANA job immediately and to become *PM*'s correspondent at an increase in salary. I was being paid a thousand dollars a month by NANA, the same sum I was re-

ceiving from CBS, and I was satisfied with the salary paid
me. I notified Ralph that I had no desire to change jobs,
but that I would keep *PM* in mind in case anyone turned
up who wanted the job he was offering.

I had written a series of articles on wheat harvesting
in Kansas for dummy issues of *PM* at the time the newspaper was being planned, and had accepted common
stock valued at twenty-five hundred dollars in lieu of
money for my services. It was not farfetched reasoning,
under stressful circumstances, to argue that I was a stock-
holder in the company that published *PM*, and that it
would be to my best interest to work for my own company. It was a difficult decision for me to make, and I
promised myself I would not make the change if somebody else could not be found to take the NANA job.
Fortunately, Eugene Petrov was anxious to become
NANA's correspondent, and he took over my work at
once. I sent Ralph a radiogram the next day telling him
that he had won his war and that I was going to work for
PM.

By the middle of September I realized that I would be
unable to maintain much longer the round-the-clock
schedule of writing for *PM* and *Life* and broadcasting
for CBS. I notified each of the companies that I had decided to leave Moscow in October and return to New
York and that arrangements should be made for others
to take over my work. Margaret had completed her final
assignment for *Life* and was ready to return to the
United States.

We arranged to get passage on a steamship in a convoy to England. It was a British convoy, and the arrangements for our passage were made by Sir Stafford Cripps, who at that time was England's ambassador to the Soviet Union. Alice-Leone Moats long before had informed Ambassador Steinhardt that she had no intention of leaving the country until she was ready to go of her own accord, and he had had to convey the message diplomatically to the Foreign Office.

I reluctantly sold my automobile and parted with my pistol-toting chauffeur and Russian secretary. It was almost equally as difficult to give up the luxurious corner suite at the National Hotel; I had become fondly attached to the winged cherubs painted in gold leaf on the ceilings. Before leaving, I sent for one final order of caviar and champagne and looked under the white bear rug and behind the pictures on the wall to make sure that no rubles had been left in their hiding places.

Early in October we went by train to Arkhangelsk, arriving there two days later at nightfall just as rain, mixed with snow and sleet, was falling. The passenger steamer we boarded had been built for service in the tropics and was not equipped with any means for heating. Besides ourselves, there were only a dozen other passengers aboard when we left for the long, cold, slow convoy trip through the White Sea and across Barents Sea and the Norwegian Sea to the Firth of Clyde. The winter fog lifted only occasionally, and then for only an hour or two at midday, and for that reason German planes were able to make few attacks on the convoy.

9.

I thought I had done a great amount of writing in five months in Russia, but the sum of it seemed insignificant in comparison with the large number of typewritten pages I produced in two weeks in England.

It seemed as though nearly every newspaper in Fleet Street had been planning since June to bid on exclusive rights to a series of feature articles on any phase of the Russian-German War. Journalistic competition at that time in London appeared to be even more aggressive and ruthless than it had been in Moscow and New York.

During the evening of the second day after we arrived in London from Glasgow, I contracted to write seven articles on the Russian-German War as I had observed it in Moscow and at the Smolensk front and I went to work that same night on the series in my room at the Savoy Hotel. Possibly to be assured of my handing each article to the right newspaper, and not to a competitor, a messenger from *The Daily Mail* was stationed in the hallway with instructions not to leave my door until I had given him the first installment. The first article in the series appeared in print the following day. In order to complete the series within the agreed-upon time, the work required the services of one full-time typist.

Before the seven articles were finished, Hutchinson and Company, publishers, asked me to expand the newspaper installments for use in a volume of photographs-

and-text. Margaret agreed to make a selection of seventy-eight of her Russian photographs for the book. I completed my work within a week and the volume was scheduled for publication in December. The title of the collaborative work was *Russia at War*.

With four days remaining before we were to leave for the United States, Hutchinson and Company offered to publish the wartime diary I had kept in Moscow. The diary consisted of hundreds of pages of notes I had made, and considerable editing was necessary; but the book was finished in four days with the assistance of two full-time typists. It was scheduled for publication the following January. The title was *Moscow under Fire*.

London itself was more bomb-devastated than Moscow, and hardship more evident, but the spirited British people were more interested in reading about what was happening in Russia than they were in talking about their own plight.

We went by plane from England to Portugal, and at Lisbon took the Yankee Clipper of Pan American World Airways to the United States. We arrived in New York the first week in November, 1941, almost exactly one month after leaving Moscow. My first trip around the world had been completed.

Freed from the pressure of deadline writing and broadcasting during the normal eighteen-hour-a-day period in Moscow, and from the severity of two weeks of concentrated work in London, I had made up mind before reaching New York that I would not rush immediately into any kind of writing in America.

However, Duell, Sloan and Pearce urged me to let them have the manuscript of a book based on my radio broadcasts and newspaper correspondence in Moscow, and to deliver it at the earliest possible moment. It was the kind of book I wished to write and, vowing not to engage in any other kind of writing until it was finished, I began work on it at once.

With the help of Mildred Zinn, who again came to Darien to help me as secretary and editorial assistant, the first few chapters were finished by the end of November. Mildred, fortunately, was able to read my scrawled pencil notes and much time was saved by my being able to use the typed copies she made of them. The book was completed by the end of December and given the title of *All-Out on the Road to Smolensk*. It was planned for publication by Duell, Sloan and Pearce in February, 1942, two months after the United States entered the Second World War.

In January, 1942, I began writing a novel based on the lively action of guerrilla warfare in the Soviet Union. The purpose of the novel was to explain, in fictional form, the part taken in the Soviet Union, during a time of war, by civilians. It seemed to me that partisan warfare, as it was called, was to become an important part of international conflict in the future and that an explanation of it would be of interest to Americans. This was the first fiction I had written, aside from short stories, since the publication of *Trouble in July* in 1940. The new novel, the title of which was *All Night Long*, was written in three and a half months in Darien and the manuscript

Call It Experience

was delivered to Duell, Sloan and Pearce in April. It was listed for publication in the early fall of 1942. *All Night Long* became a selection of the Book League of America that season and the motion-picture rights were purchased for fifty thousand dollars by Metro-Goldwyn-Mayer.

By this time I was weary and exhausted after so much activity during the preceding twelve months. As the result of a thorough physical examination, I was advised to take a vacation from writing of any nature during the remainder of the year. There had been a few times since 1925 when I was not gathering material for writing or actually writing, and I protested that I would not be able to stay away from my typewriter for seven or eight months. The physician advised me again, and more strongly this time, to follow his advice.

I phoned Harry Behn in Tucson and told him that I was ready at last to buy a home on the Arizona desert and to go there to live for a while. Harry helped me to select a newly completed house in the foothills of the Catalina Mountains eight miles north of Tucson. The rambling, flat-roofed, desert-modern house, which was built inside a high-walled patio, and which cost twenty thousand dollars, was situated in the sahuaro-covered foothills overlooking the city and Santa Cruz Valley. Across the wide valley and to the south were the lofty Santa Rita Mountains, purple and majestic in the late-afternoon shadows. I was ready to admit to Harry that I had been homesick for the desert ever since I left there in the sunshine of that morning in December of 1939.

Call It Experience

By the end of June, 1942, I was ready to leave Connecticut for the West, fully intending to be in Southern Arizona within a week.

10.

On the way to Tucson, I had planned to stop in Santa Fe for several days to visit Alfred Morang, who had moved to New Mexico from the State of Maine; Mildred Zinn, who had agreed to continue working for me as secretary and editorial assistant in Arizona, had bought our train tickets and made hotel reservations in Santa Fe, Phoenix, and Tucson. The day before we were to leave New York, I went to a cocktail party at the publishing house of Simon and Schuster in Rockefeller Center.

I arrived late at the party, and when I got there, Richard Simon said that Jake Wilk of Warner Brothers was waiting at his office to talk about something of importance. I phoned Jake and spent the next forty-five minutes trying to convince him that I was not interested in considering an offer to go to the Warner Brothers' studio in Burbank to work on the script of a motion picture.

"I've saved up to do nothing for a while, Jake," I told him. "I can afford not to work for a year."

"This is not something to take lightly," he said in a solemn voice. "The important thing is that you're wanted at the studio for this particular picture. It's my job to get you there."

"But I've got to get to Arizona, Jake. I can't go to Burbank now. Maybe some other time."

"Warner Brothers are going to film *Mission to Moscow*, the book by Joseph E. Davies, as soon as possible. There's no time to lose. The State Department is anxious to get this picture before the public for psychological reasons. You wouldn't be asked to work on this particular picture if you weren't needed. And it'd be different if you were coming to us. But we're coming to you. Now, let's talk about the details."

"But you don't understand, Jake. I've got to take a rest before I can do any kind of writing."

"The studio can't wait. We want to rush this picture into production and you're needed now. You've spent considerable time in Russia recently and you know the authentic background for the picture. That's why you've been asked to do this job. When can you leave?"

"I'm leaving on the Century tomorrow night, but I'm stopping off in Santa Fe for a few days."

"That's fine," he said enthusiastically. "It'll work out just right. Here's what I want you to promise to do. When your train gets to Kansas City, hop off and phone me at home. It'll only take a few minutes to get the call through, and The Chief stops there for twenty minutes. I'll be expecting to hear from you. Can I count on that?"

"All right, Jake," I promised. "I'll call you."

When I left the phone, it was past eight o'clock and all the other guests had gone. I went back to Darien that night wondering how I could convince Jake Wilk and

Warner Brothers that I needed a long rest from writing. Both Max Lieber and Mildred Zinn urged me the next day not to let anything keep me from going to Arizona as I had planned.

I phoned Jake Wilk from the Union Station in Kansas City and told him that I still intended to go to Tucson from Santa Fe, and not to Burbank. Jake asked me to wait another day or two before making a final decision. There was no time left for further argument, and so I told him that I would decide definitely what to do about it when I got to Santa Fe.

Two days later, in Santa Fe, I phoned Alvin G. Manuel in Beverly Hills. Al Manuel was a motion-picture agent I had met several years before and I had confidence in his judgment about anything concerning Hollywood. Al asked me how I was feeling. I told him that I was feeling better since I had got as far west as New Mexico and hoped to feel even better when I reached Southern Arizona.

"I wouldn't do that if I were you, Skinny," Al said discouragingly. "It's too hot down there on that desert in July and August. I've heard all about it. It gets up to a hundred and ten or twenty in the shade in the summertime. I'd hate to see you take that kind of beating. How much money did Jake Wilk offer you?"

I told him that there had been no discussion of salary.

"What was your last studio salary?" he asked.

I told him the amount I had received the last time I worked at the Metro-Goldwyn-Mayer studios.

"We'll improve that," Al said confidently. "We won't work for anybody for an out-of-date salary. That'd be a poor policy."

"Al, I don't think I can do it," I said. "I've got to stay away from any kind of writing for a while. I need a rest. My doctor told me so."

"Skinny, your trouble is you're hungry and don't know it. I can tell that by the way you sound on the phone. You've been hopping around all over the world for the past year and you haven't been getting enough grease in your stomach. I'm worried about you. You need to start eating right away. I've got Theodore Dreiser and Richard Aldington out here eating now, and both of them swear they've never felt better in their lives. We can do this job for Warner Brothers in a couple of months, and I'll give you my word of honor that you'll get plenty of blue-ribbon steak and greasy-fried potatoes. That sand down there in Arizona will have cooled off some by the first of November and you'll be able to walk around without scorching your feet. I'm going to take care of everything and phone you in a couple of days. Don't go away. And be thinking about those steaks. So long."

Two days later Al phoned me at La Fonda in Santa Fe and said everything had been attended to.

"What's been attended to?" I asked him.

"I've closed the deal with Warner Brothers and bought a couple of sides of that blue-ribbon beef I was talking about. The salary's going to be twelve hundred and fifty a week. Last night I sampled one of the steaks in our locker, and it's going to be all right. I'll bet you could eat a couple of charcoal-broiled New York cuts right now. When will you get here?"

"What's today?"

"Thursday."

"I'll be there Sunday."

"So long," Al said.

I went to work at Warner Brothers' studio in Burbank the following week. First I wrote an outline of the story with Robert Buckner, who was producing the picture, and then I wrote a preliminary screenplay. I felt that I had done my share of the writing and was willing to let someone else put the screenplay into final form so that I could leave for my delayed vacation in Arizona. The screenwriters who followed me insisted, for political reasons or otherwise, that I should not receive screen credit for the work I had done, and went so far as to force Warner Brothers, with the approval of The Screenwriters' Guild, to remove my name from the film. Screenwriting, like journalism and the writing of travel books, had always been subordinate to my principal interest in life and the controversy was of minor importance to me. In fact, I was pleased, considering the contribution I had made to the picture, to know that someone believed that *Mission to Moscow* film credits would be helpful to a Hollywood screenwriting career.

By the first of November I was ready to leave for Arizona. I told Mildred Zinn that I did not intend to do any writing until after the first of the year, and Mildred decided to stay in Hollywood. There was considerable correspondence to be answered, however, as well as financial records to be brought up to date, and I engaged Polly Stallsmith, whose home was in Pasadena, to go to Tucson and help me for the next few months. Polly was young and energetic, and she willingly adapted herself to the unusual hours I often kept.

It was sunset when I reached Tucson one evening in the first week of November, and I called Harry Behn and asked him to tell me how to find the house I had bought sight unseen that spring. Harry had never been to the new house after dark and we searched for it with flashlights for more than an hour. At the end of that time, after we had tramped over what seemed like a considerable area of Catalina Foothills, we decided we would have to wait to find the house by daylight.

The next morning we stopped at the office of the contractor who had built the house and asked for directions for finding my new home.

"It's very easy to find," the contractor said. "Every construction job in the Foothills is numbered. All you have to do is look for Job No. 67. That's your house."

We found the building, surrounded by three acres of spreading palo verdes and twenty-foot sahuaros, half an hour later. On a stake at the driveway entrance there was a neatly lettered sign reading "Job No. 67." It seemed like as good a name as any for a house, and so it remained.

Call It Experience

11.

After two weeks in the Tucson sun, and after having spent most of the daylight hours on the roof-top sundeck or riding horseback over the greasewood and mesquite desert, it was easy to be convinced that there was no purpose in forcing myself to stay away from the typewriter any longer.

From time to time during the past four years I had written a number of episodes of the life of a twelve-year-old boy in Georgia. Most of these chapters, written in Darien, New York, Moscow, and Santa Fe, had been published in magazines during that period. It seemed logical now that the thing to do was to complete the story of William Stroup and his friend Handsome Brown. I wrote the four concluding episodes on the sundeck during the next four weeks, finishing the book on my thirty-ninth birthday. *Georgia Boy* was published by Duell, Sloan and Pearce in April, 1943.

Shortly before Christmas, 1942, I phoned Max Lieber in New York and told him that I had become restless since finishing *Georgia Boy*. Max asked me what I was planning to do next. I told him that I had no plans but that after two months in Arizona I was feeling too good merely to sit still and do nothing. He then told me that Lee Keedick, a lecture-bureau manager, had proposed that I give a series of talks in the Middle West on the Russian-German War as I had observed it in Moscow.

Call It Experience

It seemed at the time to be a worthwhile way to spend the month of January and I told Max I would come to New York to talk about the schedule Lee Keedick had proposed.

I left Tucson on an American Airlines plane a few days later, and in New York consented to undertake a month's lecture tour under Lee Keedick's management. Engagements were immediately arranged at Joplin, Tulsa, St. Louis, Cincinnati, Toledo, Cleveland, and at Miami University, Oxford, Ohio.

The phone was ringing in my room at the St. Regis Hotel when I returned two hours after midnight after walking around in Times Square on New Year's Eve. As soon as I answered the phone, I recognized Al Manuel's voice.

"Where've you been all night?" Al said in a scolding tone. "I've been trying to get you for the past four hours."

"Is this a friendly social call?" I asked suspiciously.

"Sure," he said. "How's New Year's in New York?"

"It was all right," I said, still wondering why he had called at that time of night. "How is it in Los Angeles?"

"Don't know yet," he said. "Too early out here to tell. It's still only eleven o'clock. Hardly anybody's been killed in automobile wrecks so far. I'll let you know all about it when you get here."

"I'm not coming to Los Angeles, Al," I said right away. "I'm going to Joplin, Missouri."

"Yeh? To do what?"

"To lecture."

Call It Experience

"That's bad, Skinny," he said slowly. "I'm sorry to hear you've been thinking about such things. It's a good thing I called you in time. There's no future in that. No social security. Do you know where folks who go around the country lecturing end up?"

"Where?"

"At the Old Folks' Home. That's what it's called now. It used to be called the Poor Old Lecturing Folks' Final Home and Burial Ground."

"I've already signed a contract, Al."

"And nowadays the worn-out old lecturers who're too sad-looking for the Old Folks' Home end up on Skid Row begging for dimes. You've seen them many times. It's awfully pathetic. It's hard to believe they used to travel around the country giving lectures, isn't it?"

"But what about the contract I signed?"

"You wouldn't want to be the cause of my breaking my word of honor, would you, Skinny? You wouldn't do that to a real friend, would you? It's an awful thing for anybody in my business to lose his word of honor. It's almost as bad as being an actor and having no place to act. I gave Boris Morros and Sam Spiegle my word of honor that I'd get you to Twentieth Century–Fox the day after tomorrow at ten-thirty in the morning. They want you to do some writing on a picture they're producing. I improved your studio salary. I brought it up to date. It's going to be fifteen hundred dollars a week at Twentieth Century–Fox."

"Al, I'd have to settle my contract with Lee Keedick, if I did that. And I don't know how much that would cost. Maybe I couldn't afford it. I'd better go to Joplin."

"We don't worry about that. If we don't want to pay it, we'll let Boris and Sam take care of it. You'd better get a fast plane on TWA tomorrow. I'll have a reservation for you at the Beverly-Wilshire. And let this be a lesson to you, Skinny. Don't ever let anybody try to talk you into going to Joplin again. So long."

Before leaving New York, I gave Jed Harris a manuscript copy of *Georgia Boy* to read. I had talked to Jed several days before about the book's possibilities as a play and he had said he would like to direct and produce a dramatization of the story on Broadway during the fall of 1943. Jed said he would read the story and see me in Beverly Hills in about a month.

When Jed Harris got to the Twentieth Century–Fox studio in February, he said he was in a hurry to find a dramatist for *Georgia Boy* so he could prepare a Broadway production for an early fall opening. He then said it would save a lot of time if I would talk to Marc Connelly and persuade him to dramatize it. When I asked him why he did not speak to Marc about it, he said he was afraid that he and Marc would get into an argument about how the play should be staged and thereby endanger a friendship of long standing.

I saw Marc several times, and on each occasion, no matter what excuse I offered for Jed, he seemed to be displeased because Jed had sent me to talk about the play instead of coming himself. Finally, I told Jed that I thought we would have to look to somebody else to dramatize *Georgia Boy*.

Jed then decided that Nunnally Johnson would dramatize *Georgia Boy*. I spent several afternoons in Nunnally's office at the studio waiting for an opportunity to talk about the play. Each time Jed arrived, Damon Runyon was with him, and no one wished to do anything but listen when Damon got started on one of his long tales about Broadway. At the end of the week, the play had not been mentioned, and Jed said he had to return to New York immediately. Before he left, he assured me that Nunnally was going to write the play.

"Has Nunnally ever said he would like to dramatize the book?" I asked him.

"No, but Nunnally wants to do it," Jed said. "I'm sure of it. He'd be deeply hurt if we let anyone else dramatize it now. He's set his heart on doing it. But Nunnally's peculiar. He won't talk about something he wants very much to do. And if he doesn't want to do something, he'll talk your ears off about it. He hasn't said a word about this play, and that's how I know he's very anxious to do it."

After Jed had gone back to New York, I asked Nunnally if he expected to hear from Jed about writing a dramatization.

"No," he said. "Jed's a very peculiar person. He won't discuss something he's anxious to get me to do, and if he doesn't want me to do a particular thing, there's no way to keep him quiet."

"Did Jed say anything about dramatizing *Georgia Boy?*"

"Not a word. It's the first I've heard of it. If he had

mentioned it, I'd have known he didn't want me to do it."

"Then how can you and Jed get together on *Georgia Boy?*"

"We can't—until he stops being peculiar."

Three months later the option Jed Harris held on the dramatic rights to *Georgia Boy* expired. The contract was not renewed.

12.

It was not until 1944 that I was able to return to Tucson and begin writing the concluding novels in the series I had planned as a cyclorama of Southern life. In that year, *Tragic Ground* was published by Duell, Sloan and Pearce.

The year before, 1943, I had signed a two-year contract for screenwriting at Twentieth Century–Fox. The terms of the contract provided for a salary of seventeen hundred and fifty dollars weekly for the first year and two thousand dollars weekly for the second year. At the end of the first year I asked to be released from the agreement so that I could return to writing novels.

When I went back to Tucson in the fall of 1944, I sold the home I had lived in so infrequently during the past two years and bought a larger house in Catalina Foothills at a cost of thirty-five thousand dollars. The new house was situated at a higher altitude and it provided a better view of the Santa Cruz Valley and the Santa Rita Mountains.

Call It Experience

The first writing I did in Tucson that fall was a series of radio announcements for the War Finance Division of the Treasury Department. In November, at the request of the Treasury Department, I went on a bond-rally tour in Arizona and California with Vicki Baum, S. J. Perelman, Irving Stone, and Kathleen Winsor. The purpose of the radio announcements and the tour was to promote the sale of war bonds.

Two additional volumes of *American Folkways* were published during this time. These were *Far North Country*, by Thames Williamson, and *Deep Delta Country*, by Harnett T. Kane. Three more volumes were planned for publication in 1945, these being *Town Meeting Country*, by Clarence M. Webster, *North Star Country*, by Meridel Le Sueur, and *Golden Gate Country*, by Gertrude Atherton. The four volumes that were planned for publication in the series during the next two years, 1946 and 1947, were *Southern California Country*, by Carey McWilliams, *Lower Piedmont Country*, by H. C. Nixon, *Corn Country*, by Homer Croy, and *Big Country: Texas*, by Donald Day.

The following year in Tucson, 1945, I began writing the next novel in the series, *A House in the Uplands*, and signed a contract with Jack Kirkland for a dramatization of *Georgia Boy*. The novel was published by Duell, Sloan and Pearce a year later, and at the same time the stage production of *Georgia Boy* opened and closed within a week's time in Boston. The four concluding novels in the series were *The Sure Hand of God*, published in 1947, *This Very Earth*, published in 1948,

Call It Experience

Place Called Estherville, published in 1949, and *Episode in Palmetto*, published in 1950.

Prior to 1946 I was aware of the existence of a brash newcomer in the publishing field, but it was not until the autumn of that year that I realized how large the circulation of twenty-five-cent pocket-sized books had suddenly become. Kurt Enoch and Victor Weybright, under the imprint of Penguin Books (the name was later changed to Signet Books), had issued a quarter reprint of *God's Little Acre* early in 1946, and within six months the sale of the book had amounted to a million copies.

I went to New York in November of 1946 to attend a cocktail party given jointly by Signet Books and Fawcett Publications, the latter being the national distributors, and I was wholly skeptical of Roscoe Fawcett's prediction that the sale of *God's Little Acre* in the Signet edition would be in excess of two million copies within another six months' time. Roscoe was correct, of course, and I was wrong. The circulation of the book exceeded five million copies during the next four years.

The sales-promotion methods employed by Signet and Fawcett, while known to some extent by magazine and newspaper publishers, were radically different from those traditionally used by trade-book publishers. There were ethics involved in the distribution of quarter paperbound reprints; the ethics were to achieve mass sales regardless of buyer resistance or trade competition. I attended a number of sales conventions, as the guest of Signet and Fawcett, in New York, Colorado Springs, and elsewhere; and, in addition, in the company of Ed-

ward L. Lewis, a Fawcett sales executive, I had the opportunity to observe a number of regional promotion cam-
paigns in full flower.

The planning and execution of practical jokes appeared
to be as important to the Fawcett organization's sales
program as the writing up of orders, and I was contin-
ually on my guard whenever I was in the company of
Roscoe Fawcett or Eddie Lewis. However, as watchful
as I was, I did become the victim of one of their carefully planned schemes.

Eddie Lewis had asked me to meet him in Kansas City
promptly at noon on June 25, 1948. I drove that morning from St. Louis and reached the city limits of Kansas
City at eleven-thirty. I had gone only a block inside the
city limits when a police car containing two patrolmen,
with siren screaming, forced me to the curb. I may have
been exceeding the speed limit in a twenty-five-mile-an-
hour zone, but I was certain I was not traveling more
than thirty miles an hour. I was prepared to argue about
it, but I was not given an opportunity.

One of the policemen jotted down my license number
and looked at my driver's permit. Then he directed me
to follow the police car into town.

We were almost at the center of the city when I drove
alongside the police car and asked if I could go first to
the Muehlebach Hotel where I had an important business
appointment. The policemen said we would go there
first.

I drove up to the entrance of the Muehlebach a few
minutes before twelve o'clock, the police car directly

behind me, and Eddie Lewis was waiting at the doorway for me.

"There's no time to waste, Erskine," Eddie said excitedly. "We've got to hurry to keep an important appointment I made for us."

I nodded toward the police car and told him that I had been arrested for speeding.

Eddie shook his head worriedly. "That's bad," he said. "I wonder what we ought to do." He thought for several moments before speaking again. "We'd better go see the mayor." He grabbed me by the arm and pushed me into a taxi.

As we started off, I looked through the rear window and saw the police car following us closely. Several times during the ride to City Hall, I tried to speak about the traffic charge against me, but Eddie managed to maintain a conversation on other subjects. When we reached City Hall, the two policemen followed us into the building and walked into the mayor's office behind us.

A moment later, Eddie and I were standing before Mayor William Kemp and I was being presented with a scroll of welcome to Kansas City. After thanking Mayor Kemp for the honor, I nudged Eddie with my elbow and whispered something about the traffic charge against me. Eddie leaned forward and said something to Mayor Kemp.

"Do you have something there for Mr. Caldwell?" the mayor asked the policemen.

One of them stepped forward, grinning, and handed me a slip of yellow paper. On it was printed the words,

Call It Experience

"Welcome to Kansas City, Missouri! Please drive carefully!"

Afterward, Eddie would never admit that he had planned any part of the affair other than the appointment with Mayor Kemp. However, when he went back to the home office in Greenwich, Connecticut, he told Roscoe Fawcett that the Kansas City promotion campaign was one of the most successful he had ever directed.

After leaving Kansas City, where I finished my part in the promotion campaign by autographing quarter books in a Katz Drugstore, I went to the University of Kansas, in Lawrence, to spend a week at a writers' conference being held in conjunction with the university summer school. There were a number of authors in attendance, and from the beginning I noticed an unmistakable atmosphere of coolness each time I appeared at one of the meetings. I did not know the cause of this until I asked Walter Van Tilburg Clark, one of the authors at the conference, if I had affronted anyone. Walter said he had heard that some of the other authors were displeased because they felt that I had brought disrepute to the profession of authorship—and to the cause of higher education, as well—by participating in such an undignified publicity scheme in Kansas City, and by autographing twenty-five-cent books in a drugstore.

Epilogue

I.

Whenever anyone who professes to have the ambition to be a writer comes to an author for help and advice, there are several questions that generally can be expected to be heard. The two questions, spoken and written, most frequently asked of me are:

How do you write a story?
How do you get a story published?

After all these years I still do not know how to answer these questions to the complete satisfaction of curious readers and eager young writers. Evidently most of them think I am withholding a secret, because few are satisfied with my answer. The reply I usually make is that it has been my experience that the best way to learn to write is by writing and that the best way to get a story published is to send it to magazines until an editor is found who is willing to accept it for publication.

Housewives in Texas, taxi drivers in Ohio, students in Nebraska, and clerks in California who have received such replies from me could rightfully complain that I failed to give clear and ample instructions for finding the how of writing and publication. Perhaps the reason

Call It Experience

I am unable to give explicit directions that would assure anyone of becoming a successful writer is because I consider creative writing to be motivated by a certain state of mind; and believe that only those who are born with the gift or who acquire the indefinable urge to express themselves in print can accomplish it.

This state of mind, as I call it, is an almost uncontrollable desire that seeks fulfillment at any cost. It is a craving that will not be denied. It is similar to the emotional need, as some find it, to seek love and companionship; to others it is as overpowering as the physical necessity for food and drink. The intensity of this state of mind forces a person onward to whatever extent he is willing to go in order to achieve his conscious, or subconscious, goal in life.

The degree of intensity of this state of mind is the measure of success or failure. Many persons are willing to undergo almost any human hardship in order to learn how to write successfully. Others, easily discouraged, find logical excuses for giving up and turning to another occupation. Just as there are these two extremes, there are also, and in greater number, those who yearn to be writers and yet lack the necessary ability to succeed.

It is often believed by many persons who have lived through long years of learning the craft of writing that those who willingly endure hardships are the ones most likely to succeed as creative writers. It would be foolish to maintain that a person must be penniless in order to fit himself for authorship, but it is true that the desire to be a writer is composed of, for one thing, a spirit of aggressiveness that impels a man or woman to strive to overcome anything that stands in the way of success. More common than wealth and ease, poverty and hunger are both symbolic and real, and the would-be writer is encouraged to greater effort as he sees himself gradually overcoming them. The same person, perhaps with similar talent, though born to wealth, is likely to direct his aggressiveness toward the goal of gaining such ends as fame and achievement as a man of letters. The reward of accomplishment, in the mind of the majority of authors, rich or poor, is the primary motive for writing, and the making of money is a secondary one.

I have rarely hesitated to discourage a person who says that he lacks the leisure to write, or that editors fail to appreciate his work. Such an attitude may seem to be unsympathetic, yet I feel that it is honest and realistic, and consequently more beneficial than bland encouragement. Many would-be writers, perhaps unconsciously, are seeking excuses for not continuing to struggle for success, and they will live a happier existence and be more useful as citizens in an occupation other than writing. A person with the will to write can always find the opportunity; those who are not inclined to seek the opportunity usually have other interests, whether they know it or not, that are more dear to them.

Many who attempt to write fiction, either as a pastime or as a profession, would be more successful if they had a better understanding of the nature of what they are trying to do. There are many definitions of fiction. My definition of a short story or novel is that it is an imaginary tale with a meaning, interesting enough to hold a reader's attention, and profound enough to leave a lasting impression on his mind. There are probably so-called natural-born storytellers, but I hold that the greater number of fiction writers acquire, either by diligent practice or by intelligent instruction, the ability to create a story with a completeness that will interest persons other than the author. And, if enough persons become interested, it is reasonable to expect that at least one of them will be the editor of a magazine.

Probably all authors possess a native ability to some degree in the beginning, even if the talent is no more than that of having the mental capacity to distinguish one word from another, but it is doubtful if anyone who has published a short story or novel attained that distinction without first serving an apprenticeship, lengthy or brief, but certainly of some duration.

This period of going to school to fiction, combined with the state of mind which results in one becoming an accomplished storyteller, draws to the surface whatever talent the writer possesses. Impatience, inadequate apprenticeship, or unwillingness to sit at a typewriter day after day and year after year may well outweigh the most intense state of mind or will to succeed. When this occurs, the desire to write may remain, but the ability is weak and ineffectual. What follows then is likely to be frustration and unhappiness.

Stories and novels are being written now and will

continue to be written. Many of the new writers will be men and women of all ages who discover that one of the secrets of writing is in learning by practice how to express thought and feeling, and who practice until the stories they write are so good that readers wish to read them and magazines wish to publish them.

2.

Every author receives both fan mail and pan mail in varying quantity and proportion. In my case the proportion of friendly letters and unfriendly letters has come to be about nine of the former to one of the latter. Since 1929 when my first story appeared in print, the average number of such letters received has been at least ten weekly. In twenty years, this amounted to approximately ten thousand letters, their messages ranging from unstinted praise to utter damnation. I have not had the time, or in some instances the inclination, to reply to as many as half of them. About one third of the mail I receive can be counted on to make a request for money, for an autograph, and for advice concerning personal and professional problems.

The questions that follow, similarly worded in effect, are typical of those most frequently asked by readers. Likewise, many of them are also the most popular questions asked by students, reporters, and other persons professing interest in the professional life and working habits of a writer.

Call It Experience

Q: My friends tell me that I have a very interesting life story, and I think so, too. There's never been anything like it in moving pictures or a book. Will you write it if I furnish you with all the facts?

A: No. You should write your own life story. This is a form of self-expression that is valuable to you. You will derive more satisfaction from it by writing it yourself.

Q: I can tell you a story which I'm convinced will make a lot of money when it is put into a novel. I thought it up myself and nobody else knows it. Will you collaborate with me for half the royalties?

A: No. Fiction is the product of an individual's mind and emotions and it is most successful when it is written by the one who creates it.

Q: Did you go to school to learn what you know about writing stories and books?

A: No. I learned by experience, by trial-and-error. And by working at it until I was satisfied with the result.

Q: I have written several short stories in my spare time. How can I get them published?

A: By sending them to magazines. Not merely to one or two magazines, but to hundreds of them if necessary. Any bookshop can obtain for you a copy of a book with the names and addresses of magazines that publish short stories. This is the most satisfactory way to bring your work to the attention of editors.

Call It Experience

After you have had your first story published, a literary agent may be of help to you.

Q: Do the characters in your stories and novels really exist? Are they real people?

A: No. They are fictional characters. I strive to make imaginary people true to life.

Q: A man in one of your books talks and behaves just like my uncle. Were you really writing about him?

A: No. But I am always pleased to find that one of my fictional characters has a counterpart in actual life.

Q: What is your purpose in writing books like *Tobacco Road*, *Journeyman*, and *Tragic Ground*? What good do such books do?

A: The purpose of all the books of fiction I have written is to provide a mirror into which people may look. Whatever good or harm my books do depends upon an individual's reaction to the image he sees in the mirror.

Q: You write too much about poor people. Why don't you write about the pleasant things in life?

A: Those enjoying the pleasant things in life are fewer than those enduring the unpleasant. When this social condition no longer exists, I'll feel there is no longer any purpose in writing about the effects of poverty on the human spirit.

Q: Only somebody with a mind like yours would

write a book like *God's Little Acre*. Are you crazy?

A: I don't consider myself so. My reactions appear to me to be normal.

Q: I have submitted my short stories to all the leading magazines, but I still haven't been able to get one published. I'm beginning to be discouraged. What should I do?

A: There's always room for one more good writer at the top, and the best way to get there is to start at the bottom. If you are not interested in beginning at the bottom, you are probably not particularly interested in writing as a career. However, there are thousands of weekly newspapers, trade journals, little magazines, and specialized publications of every description. It seems reasonable to believe that anyone with sufficient determination and patience, and with some degree of writing ability, can find acceptance somewhere among all these publications. If the important thing in your life is to get your work into print, it will look good to you no matter where it appears. And if it looks good to readers, too, you'll find that there are editors and publishers who will wish to help you along the way to the top.

Q: Will I be able to learn how to write short stories and novels by taking a course in a school or university?

A: No one can say until you try. No honest teacher would promise to make a writer of you, but instruction will help you to help yourself.

Call It Experience

Q: I want to be a short-story writer. Will working as a reporter on a newspaper be helpful or harmful?

A: I have never known anyone to be harmed by the practice of any kind of writing. In addition to giving you the benefit of constant practice, journalism will help you to form the habit of writing every day. Waiting-for-inspiration is an excuse rarely found among newspaper-trained authors.

Q: I've always wanted to write, but I have a family to support and I can't give up my job and take a chance on making a living by writing. What should I do?

A: Do both. Keep your job and write. Not all published writers are professional writers. Much good work is done by those who are forced by circumstances to do housework every day or to go to business five or six days a week. Writing, like stamp collecting and trapshooting, can be an interesting hobby, and few stamp collectors or trapshooters give up their jobs.

Q: Do you write to make money?

A: I write because I like to write. I would be unable to devote all my time to writing if I could not make a living from the practice of my profession.

Q: How much money do you make?

A: I have no stable income. My income is derived from royalties and payments for writing. I have earned as little as ten dollars a year and as much as three thousand dollars a week.

Q: I've heard that you made a million dollars from your writing. Do you still have it?

A: No. Three fourths of my income is consumed by personal and professional expenses and by taxes.

Q: Do you have regular working hours, or do you write when you feel like it?

A: I work from nine a.m. to five p.m., six days a week, ten months a year.

Q: Do you actually write all the time you are working?

A: No. But I sit at the typewriter just the same. There have been times when I had not written a single line by the end of the day.

Q: Do you ever rewrite your stories and novels, or is everything the way you want it the first time?

A: My wastebasket is always full at the end of the day. I've rewritten stories and novels as many as ten or twelve times.

Q: There must be some one thing that you consider the most important element of your writing. What is it?

A: Not using a word of many syllables when a shorter word will do. Not using a word that has to be looked up in a dictionary for definition or for spelling. Once

I revised my copy of the dictionary by striking out all the words in it that had more than four syllables.

Q: What do you consider the most important steps in learning to write?

A: First, learn the meaning and usage of words; second, learn how to construct a sentence to convey a desired thought; third, have something worthwhile to say before beginning a story; fourth, learn how to employ the emotional force of a story to produce lasting impressions upon the mind of the reader.

Q: What advice would you give a young writer?

A: Fit yourself for writing to the extent that anyone who desires to become successful in his field undergoes a period of apprenticeship. Doctors, lawyers, bakers, barbers, mechanics, engineers, and printers must learn by experience. Why shouldn't writers?

Q: What books do you read?

A: I read few books. Perhaps half a dozen novels a year. Many years ago I divided the population into two parts: those who read and those who write. I wished to belong in the latter category.

Q: If you had your life to live over, would you start out to be a writer again?

A: I most certainly would. I doubt if I could make a living doing anything else.